*Current*
**CONTROVERSIES**

# The World Economy

# Other Books in the Current Controversies Series

Current
CONTROVERSIES

# The World Economy

*Noël Merino, Book Editor*

**GREENHAVEN PRESS**
*A part of Gale, Cengage Learning*

GALE
CENGAGE Learning™

Detroit • New York • San Francisco • New Haven, Conn • Waterville, Maine • London

Christine Nasso, *Publisher*
Elizabeth Des Chenes, *Managing Editor*

© 2010 Greenhaven Press, a part of Gale, Cengage Learning

Gale and Greenhaven Press are registered trademarks used herein under license.

*For more information, contact:*
Greenhaven Press
27500 Drake Rd.
Farmington Hills, MI 48331-3535
Or you can visit our Internet site at gale.cengage.com

For product information and technology assistance, contact us at

Gale Customer Support, 1-800-877-4253
For permission to use material from this text or product, submit all requests online at www.cengage.com/permissions

Further permissions questions can be emailed to permissionrequest@cengage.com

Articles in Greenhaven Press anthologies are often edited for length to meet page requirements. In addition, original titles of these works are changed to clearly present the main thesis and to explicitly indicate the author's opinion. Every effort is made to ensure that Greenhaven Press accurately reflects the original intent of the authors. Every effort has been made to trace the owners of copyrighted material.

Cover image copyright Paul Paladin, 2009. Used under license from Shutterstock.com.

**LIBRARY OF CONGRESS CATALOGING-IN-PUBLICATION DATA**

The World Economy / Noël Merino, book editor.
    p. cm. -- (Current controversies)
    Includes bibliographical references and index.
    ISBN 978-0-7377-4713-3 (hardcover) -- ISBN 978-0-7377-4714-0 (pbk.)
    1. Financial crises. 2. Globalization I. Merino, Noël.
    HB3722.W67 2010
    330.9--dc22
                                                        2009046683

Printed in the United States of America
1 2 3 4 5 6 7 14 13 12 11 10

# Contents

## Chapter 2: What Should Be Done About the Global Financial Crisis?

# Foreword

By definition, controversies are "discussions of questions in which opposing opinions clash" (Webster's Twentieth Century Dictionary Unabridged). Few would deny that controversies are a pervasive part of the human condition and exist on virtually every level of human enterprise. Controversies transpire between individuals and among groups, within nations and between nations. Controversies supply the grist necessary for progress by providing challenges and challengers to the status quo. They also create atmospheres where strife and warfare can flourish. A world without controversies would be a peaceful world; but it also would be, by and large, static and prosaic.

## The Series' Purpose

The purpose of the Current Controversies series is to explore many of the social, political, and economic controversies dominating the national and international scenes today. Titles selected for inclusion in the series are highly focused and specific. For example, from the larger category of criminal justice, Current Controversies deals with specific topics such as police brutality, gun control, white collar crime, and others. The debates in Current Controversies also are presented in a useful, timeless fashion. Articles and book excerpts included in each title are selected if they contribute valuable, long-range ideas to the overall debate. And wherever possible, current information is enhanced with historical documents and other relevant materials. Thus, while individual titles are current in focus, every effort is made to ensure that they will not become quickly outdated. Books in the Current Controversies series will remain important resources for librarians, teachers, and students for many years.

In addition to keeping the titles focused and specific, great care is taken in the editorial format of each book in the series. Book introductions and chapter prefaces are offered to provide background material for readers. Chapters are organized around several key questions that are answered with diverse opinions representing all points on the political spectrum. Materials in each chapter include opinions in which authors clearly disagree as well as alternative opinions in which authors may agree on a broader issue but disagree on the possible solutions. In this way, the content of each volume in Current Controversies mirrors the mosaic of opinions encountered in society. Readers will quickly realize that there are many viable answers to these complex issues. By questioning each author's conclusions, students and casual readers can begin to develop the critical thinking skills so important to evaluating opinionated material.

Current Controversies is also ideal for controlled research. Each anthology in the series is composed of primary sources taken from a wide gamut of informational categories including periodicals, newspapers, books, U.S. and foreign government documents, and the publications of private and public organizations. Readers will find factual support for reports, debates, and research papers covering all areas of important issues. In addition, an annotated table of contents, an index, a book and periodical bibliography, and a list of organizations to contact are included in each book to expedite further research.

Perhaps more than ever before in history, people are confronted with diverse and contradictory information. During the Persian Gulf War, for example, the public was not only treated to minute-to-minute coverage of the war, it was also inundated with critiques of the coverage and countless analyses of the factors motivating U.S. involvement. Being able to sort through the plethora of opinions accompanying today's major issues, and to draw one's own conclusions, can be a complicated and frustrating struggle. It is the editors' hope that Current Controversies will help readers with this struggle.

# Introduction

*"The increase in globalization over the past several decades has made the state of the world economy as important to nations, if not more important, than their national economies, as nations become increasingly interdependent through the activities of globalization."*

An economy is the economic activities in a certain area. The economic activities that make up an economy include the production, distribution, and consumption of goods and services. One can look at the economy of a small region, such as northern California, or of a nation, such as the United States. The world economy, or global economy, encompasses all economic activities of all nations of the world. Unique issues of the world economy center on the way national economies are interrelated, through trade and foreign investment, for example. The increase in globalization over the past several decades has made the state of the world economy as important to nations, if not more important, than their national economies, as nations become increasingly interdependent through the activities of globalization.

Compared to the economies of nations today, early economies of the world were small due to limitations on human movement and, hence, limitations on movement of goods. Nonetheless, humans have been trading goods and services with each other throughout history. As travel distances increased, so did the trade of goods and services. Approximately two thousand years ago, for example, the Roman Empire established trade routes by boat between Europe and the Far East. Such trading enabled both the Romans and the Chinese to increase the market for their goods and to have the opportunity to consume goods not available in their respective countries. As transportation developed, so did trade. In American grocery stores today, for instance, there are products from all around the world brought by sea or by air, with many products arriving from overseas within one day of leaving their home country.

One of the debates about trade within the world economy is the extent to which countries should protect their national economies. For example, to protect sugar produced in the United States, is the United States justified in imposing tariffs—or fees—on imported sugar? In fact, the United States has utilized protectionistic policies toward its sugar growers for several decades, including tariffs on imported sugar, government subsidies to sugar growers, and import quotas limiting the import of foreign sugar. A February 2009 report by McKeany-Flavell, for the American Sugar Alliance, argued that the easing of restrictions on sugar imports could result in problems with quality, supply, and cost, concluding that "there is an intrinsic value provided by our domestic sugar industry." In contrast, the *Wall Street Journal*, in an August 22, 2009, editorial argued that the protectionistic program toward the U.S. sugar industry "distorts trade and has negative economic consequences." There is fierce debate about the extent to which free trade policies hurt national economies and whether or not protectionism is ever justified.

The impulse of national economies to act in ways that are protectionistic is an understandable one: Nations do not pursue trade with others to help out the other nations, but want trade to be in their own best interests. Nations pursue policies that protect their own economies in part to shield themselves from the impact of adverse events in other economies. The recent global economic crisis is one example of an event that started in one country, the United States, and quickly spread to other countries around the world because of the way in which their national economies had become intertwined with the U.S. economy. Nations want their involvement in the global economy to offer as many benefits as possible while minimizing risk to their own national economies.

Another reason for protectionism is the desire to protect the wealth of people within nations, especially within the relatively wealthy countries of the world. This growth of a world economy has been credited with increasing the wealth of the people of the world overall, but this does not mean that each individual person has seen their wealth increase. Regarding world trade, Burton G. Malkiel noted in a February 5, 2009, opinion piece for the *Wall Street Journal*, "such trade does not make everyone better off, and that is why free trade is often a tough sell, especially during times of hardship." Many people in the United States, for instance, are worried that an increase in free trade as a result of the globalization of the world economy could take their jobs overseas or result in lower wages due to competition from international workers.

As the capacity for swift, widespread trade throughout the world has increased, the world economy has been able to expand, with constituent national economies further intertwined with each other. Yet, the debate rages about whether this development has been a good one and how nations should respond to changes in the world economy. By presenting different views on the state of the world economy, including the causes of and solutions to the recent global financial crisis, and the extent to which the globalization of the world economy is good for the United States and other nations, *Current Controversies: The World Economy* helps to illuminate some of the most pressing issues surrounding current world economic activities.

*Current*
**CONTROVERSIES**

CHAPTER 1

# What Caused the Global Financial Crisis?

# Overview: The Global Financial Crisis

*International Monetary Fund*

*The International Monetary Fund is an organization of countries that works to foster global monetary cooperation, secure financial stability, facilitate international trade, promote high employment and sustainable economic growth, and reduce poverty around the world.*

In the year following the outbreak of the U.S. subprime [borrowers with poor credit] crisis in August 2007, the global economy bent but did not buckle. Activity slowed in the face of tightening credit conditions, with advanced economies falling into mild recessions by the middle quarters of 2008, but with emerging and developing economies continuing to grow at fairly robust rates by past standards. However, financial wounds continued to fester, despite policy makers' efforts to sustain market liquidity and capitalization, as concerns about losses from bad assets increasingly raised questions about the solvency and funding of core financial institutions.

## The Financial Crisis

The situation deteriorated rapidly after the dramatic blowout of the financial crisis in September 2008, following the default by a large U.S. investment bank (Lehman Brothers), the rescue of the largest U.S. insurance company (American International Group, AIG), and intervention in a range of other systemic institutions in the United States and Europe. These events promoted a huge increase in perceived counterparty risk [default risk] as banks faced large write-downs [reduction

International Monetary Fund, "Chapter 1. Global Prospects and Policies: How Did Things Get So Bad, So Fast?" *World Economic Outlook: Crisis and Recovery*, April 2009. © 2009 International Monetary Fund. Republished with permission of International Monetary Fund, conveyed through Copyright Clearance Center, Inc.

in book value], the solvency of many of the most established financial names came into question, the demand for liquidity [assets easily converted into cash] jumped to new heights, and market volatility surged once more. The result was a flight to quality that depressed yields on the most liquid government securities and an evaporation of wholesale funding that prompted a disorderly deleveraging [paying off debt] that cascaded across the rest of the global financial system. Liquid assets were sold at fire-sale prices and credit lines to hedge funds [speculative investments] and other leveraged [more debt than equity] financial intermediaries in the so-called shadow banking system were slashed. High-grade as well as high-yield corporate bond spreads [the difference between bidding and asking price] widened sharply, the flow of trade finance and working capital was heavily disrupted, banks tightened lending standards further, and equity [stock] prices fell steeply.

---

*Sharp falls in equity markets as well as continuing deflation of housing bubbles have led to a massive loss of household wealth.*

---

Emerging markets—which earlier had been relatively sheltered from financial strains by their limited exposure to the U.S. subprime market—have been hit hard by these events. New securities issues [new financial investments] came to a virtual stop, bank-related flows were curtailed, bond spreads soared, equity prices dropped, and exchange markets came under heavy pressure. Beyond a general rise in risk aversion, capital flows have been curtailed by a range of adverse factors, including the damage done to banks (especially in Western Europe) and hedge funds, which had previously been major conduits; the desire to move funds under the "umbrella" offered by the increasing provision of guarantees in mature markets; and rising concerns about national economic prospects, particularly in economies that previously had relied extensively on external financing. Adding to the strains, the turbulence exposed internal vulnerabilities within many emerging economies, bringing attention to currency mismatches on borrower balance sheets, weak risk management (for example, substantial corporate losses on currency derivatives markets in some countries), and excessively rapid bank credit growth.

## The Impact of the Crisis

Although a global meltdown was averted by determined firefighting efforts, this sharp escalation of financial stress battered the global economy through a range of channels. The credit crunch generated by deleveraging pressures and a breakdown of securitization [combining financial assets] technology has hurt even the most highly rated private borrowers. Sharp falls in equity markets as well as continuing deflation of housing bubbles have led to a massive loss of household wealth. In part, these developments reflected the inevitable adjustments to correct past excesses and technological failures akin to those that triggered the bursting of the dot-com bubble. However, because the excesses and failures were at the core of the banking system, the ramifications have been quickly transmitted to all sectors and countries of the global economy. Moreover, the scale of the blows has been greatly magnified by the collapse of business and consumer confidence in the face of rising doubts about economic prospects and continuing uncertainty about policy responses. The rapidly deteriorating economic outlook further accentuated financial strains in a corrosive global feedback loop that has undermined policy makers' efforts to remedy the situation.

Thus, the impact on activity was felt quickly and broadly. Industrial production and merchandise trade plummeted in the fourth quarter of 2008 and continued to fall rapidly in early 2009 across both advanced and emerging economies, as purchases of investment goods and consumer durables such as autos and electronics were hit by credit disruptions and rising anxiety and inventories started to build rapidly. Recent data provide some tentative indications that the rate of contraction may now [April 2009] be starting to moderate. Business confidence has picked up modestly, and there are signs that consumer purchases are stabilizing, helped by the cushion provided by falling commodity prices and anticipation of macroeconomic policy support. However, employment continues to drop fast, notably in the United States.

## Damage to World Economies

Overall, global GDP [gross domestic product] is estimated to have contracted by an alarming 6¼ percent (annualized) in the fourth quarter of 2008 (a swing from 4 percent growth one year earlier) and to have fallen almost as fast in the first quarter of 2009. All economies around the world have been seriously affected, although the direction of the blows has varied. . . . The advanced economies experienced an unprecedented 7½ percent decline in the fourth quarter of 2008, and most are now suffering deep recessions. While the U.S. economy may have suffered particularly from intensified financial strains and the continued fall in the housing sector, Western Europe and advanced Asia have been hit hard by the collapse in trade as well as rising financial problems of their own and housing corrections in some national markets.

---

*In parallel with the rapid cooling of global activity, inflation pressures have subsided quickly.*

---

Emerging economies too have suffered badly and contracted 4 percent in the fourth quarter in the aggregate. The damage has been inflicted through both financial and trade channels. Activity in east Asian economies with heavy reliance on manufacturing exports has fallen sharply, although the downturns in China and India have been somewhat muted given the lower shares of their export sectors in domestic production and more resilient domestic demand. Emerging Europe and the Commonwealth of Independent States (CIS) have been hit very hard because of heavy dependence on external financing as well as on manufacturing exports and, for the CIS, commodity exports. Countries in Africa, Latin America, and the Middle East have suffered from plummeting commodity prices as well as financial strains and weak export demand.

## Inflation and Currencies

In parallel with the rapid cooling of global activity, inflation pressures have subsided quickly. Commodity prices fell sharply from mid-year highs, undercut by the weakening prospects for the emerging economies that have provided the bulk of demand growth in recent years. At the same time, rising economic slack has contained wage increases and eroded profit margins. As a result, 12-month headline inflation in the advanced economies fell below 1 percent in February 2009 although core inflation [excluding items with volatile price movement] remained in the 1½–2 percent range with the notable exception of Japan. Inflation has also moderated significantly across the emerging economies, although in some cases falling exchange rates have moderated the downward momentum.

---

*Policy responses to these developments have been rapid, wide-ranging, and frequently unorthodox, but were too often piecemeal and have failed to arrest the downward spiral.*

---

One side effect of the financial crisis has been a flight to safety and rising home bias [bias toward domestic investment]. Gross global capital flows contracted sharply in the fourth quarter of 2008. In net terms, flows have favored countries with the most liquid and safe government securities markets, and net private flows to emerging and developing economies have collapsed. These shifts have affected the world's major currencies. Since September 2008, the euro, U.S. dollar, and yen have appreciated notably. The Chinese renminbi and other currencies pegged to the dollar (including those in the Middle East) have also appreciated in real effective terms. Most other emerging economy currencies have weakened sharply, despite use of international reserves for support.

## Policies Fail to Gain Traction

Policy responses to these developments have been rapid, wide-ranging, and frequently unorthodox, but were too often piecemeal and have failed to arrest the downward spiral. Following the heavy fallout from the collapse of Lehman Brothers, authorities in major mature markets made clear that no other potentially systemic financial institution would be allowed to fail. A number of major banks in the United States and Europe were provided with public support in the form of new capital and guarantees against losses from holdings of problem assets. More broadly, authorities have followed multifaceted strategies involving continued provision of liquidity and extended guarantees of bank liabilities to alleviate funding pressures, making available public funds for bank recapitalization, and announcing programs to deal with distressed assets. However, policy announcements have often been short on detail and have not convinced markets; cross-border coordination of initiatives has been lacking, resulting in undesirable spillovers; and progress in alleviating uncertainty related to distressed assets has been limited.

At the same time, with inflation concerns dwindling and risks to the outlook deepening, central banks have used a range of conventional and unconventional policy tools to support the economy and ease credit market conditions. Policy rates have been cut sharply, bringing them to ½ percent or less in some countries (Canada, Japan, United Kingdom, United States) and to unprecedented lows in other cases (including the euro area and Sweden). However, the impact of rate cuts has been limited by credit market disruptions, and the zero bound has constrained central bankers' ability to add further stimulus. Some central banks (notably, in Japan, United Kingdom, United States) have therefore increased purchases of long-term government securities and provided direct support to illiquid credit markets by providing funding and guarantees to intermediaries in targeted markets, with some success in bringing down spreads in specific market segments such as the U.S. commercial paper and residential mortgage-backed securities markets. As a result, central bank balance sheets have expanded rapidly as central banks have become major intermediaries in the credit process. Nevertheless, overall credit growth to the private sector has dropped sharply, reflecting a combination of tighter bank lending standards, securities market disruptions, and lower credit demand as economic prospects have darkened.

## Government Fiscal Policy

As concerns about the extent of the downturn and the limits to monetary policy have mounted, governments have also turned to fiscal policy to support demand. Beyond letting automatic stabilizers work, large discretionary stimulus packages have been introduced in most advanced economies, notably Germany, Japan, Korea, the United Kingdom, and the United States. Although the impact of the downturn and stimulus will be felt mainly in 2009 and 2010, fiscal deficits in the major advanced economies rose by more than 2 percentage points in 2008, after several years of consolidation. Government debt levels are also being boosted by public support to the banking system, and some countries' room for fiscal action has been reduced by upward pressure on government bond yields as concerns about long-term fiscal sustainability have risen.

Policy responses in the emerging and developing economies to weakening activity and rising external pressures have varied considerably, depending on circumstances. Many countries, especially in Asia and Latin America, have been able to use policy buffers to alleviate pressures, letting exchange rates adjust downward but also applying reserves to counter disorderly market conditions and to augment private credit, including in particular to sustain trade finance. Dollar swap facilities offered by the Federal Reserve [the central banking system in the United States] to a number of systemically important countries as well as the introduction of a more flexible credit instrument by the IMF [International Monetary Fund] provided some assurance to markets that countries with sound management would have access to needed external funding and not be faced with a capital account crisis. Moreover, many central banks changed course to lower policy interest rates to ease domestic conditions, as earlier inflation concerns moderated. Governments have also provided fiscal support through automatic stabilizers and discretionary measures, albeit typically on a much smaller scale than in the advanced economies, with the notable exceptions of China and Saudi Arabia. They have had room to maneuver because of their reserve stockpiles, more credible inflation-targeting regimes, and stronger public balance sheets.

Elsewhere, however, especially in emerging Europe and the CIS, greater internal vulnerabilities, and in some cases less flexible exchange rate regimes, have complicated the policy response. A number of countries that face severe external financing shortages, fragile banking systems, currency mismatches on borrower balance sheets, and rising questions about public finances have acted to tighten macroeconomic policies and received external financial support from the IMF and other official sources. However, stabilization has been elusive as the external environment has continued to deteriorate.

# Financial Deregulation Caused the Financial Crisis

*Essential Information and Consumer Education Foundation*

*The Consumer Education Foundation is a California-based non-profit, nonpartisan consumer research, education, and advocacy organization. Essential Information is a nonprofit, tax-exempt organization involved in a variety of projects that promote a more just economy, improved public health, and a sustainable planet.*

Blame Wall Street for the current financial crisis [March 2009]. Investment banks, hedge funds, and commercial banks made reckless bets using borrowed money. They created and trafficked in exotic investment vehicles that even top Wall Street executives—not to mention firm directors—did not understand. They hid risky investments in off-balance-sheet vehicles or capitalized on their legal status to cloak investments altogether. They engaged in unconscionable predatory lending that offered huge profits for a time, but led to dire consequences when the loans proved unpayable. And they created, maintained and justified a housing bubble, the bursting of which has thrown the United States and the world into a deep recession, resulting in a foreclosure epidemic ripping apart communities across the country.

But while Wall Street is culpable for the financial crisis and global recession, others do share responsibility.

## The Post-Depression Regulatory System

For the last three decades, financial regulators, Congress, and the executive branch have steadily eroded the regulatory system that restrained the financial sector from acting on its own

Robert Weissman and James Donahue, "Executive Summary," *Sold Out: How Wall Street and Washington Betrayed America*, Essential Information and Consumer Education Foundation, March 2009. Reproduced by permission of the publishers.

worst tendencies. The post-Depression regulatory system aimed to force disclosure of publicly relevant financial information; established limits on the use of leverage [using debt to finance assets]; drew bright lines between different kinds of financial activity and protected regulated commercial banking from investment bank-style risk taking; enforced meaningful limits on economic concentration, especially in the banking sector; provided meaningful consumer protections (including restrictions on usurious [very high] interest rates); and contained the financial sector so that it remained subordinate to the real economy. This hodgepodge regulatory system was, of course, highly imperfect, . . . because it too often failed to deliver on its promises.

---

*Financial deregulation led directly to the financial meltdown.*

---

But it was not its imperfections that led to the erosion and collapse of that regulatory system. It was a concerted effort by Wall Street, steadily gaining momentum until it reached fever pitch in the late 1990s and continued right through the first half of 2008. Even now, Wall Street continues to defend many of its worst practices. Though it bows to the political reality that new regulation is coming, it aims to reduce the scope and importance of that regulation and, if possible, use the guise of regulation to further remove public controls over its operations.

## The Cause of Financial Deregulation

This report has one overriding message: Financial deregulation led directly to the financial meltdown.

It also has two other, top-tier messages. First, the details matter. The report documents a dozen specific deregulatory steps (including failures to regulate and failures to enforce existing regulations) that enabled Wall Street to crash the financial system. Second, Wall Street didn't obtain these regulatory abeyances based on the force of its arguments. At every step, critics warned of the dangers of further deregulation. Their evidence-based claims could not offset the political and economic muscle of Wall Street. The financial sector showered campaign contributions on politicians from both parties, invested heavily in a legion of lobbyists, paid academics and think tanks to justify their preferred policy positions, and cultivated a pliant media—especially a cheerleading business media complex. . . .

## The Change in Bank Practices

These are the 12 Deregulatory Steps to Financial Meltdown:

*1. Repeal of the Glass-Steagall Act and the Rise of the Culture of Recklessness.* The Financial Services Modernization Act of 1999 formally repealed the Glass-Steagall Act of 1933 (also known as the Banking Act of 1933) and related laws, which prohibited commercial banks from offering investment banking and insurance services. In a form of corporate civil disobedience, Citibank and insurance giant Travelers Group merged in 1998—a move that was illegal at the time, but for which they were given a two-year forbearance—on the assumption that they would be able to force a change in the relevant law at a future date. They did. The 1999 repeal of Glass-Steagall helped create the conditions in which banks invested monies from checking and savings accounts into creative financial instruments such as mortgage-backed securities [financial assets] and credit default swaps [CDSs], investment gambles that rocked the financial markets in 2008.

*2. Hiding Liabilities: Off-Balance Sheet Accounting.* Holding assets off the balance sheet generally allows companies to exclude "toxic" or money-losing assets from financial disclosures to investors in order to make the company appear more valuable than it is. Banks used off-balance sheet operations— special purpose entities (SPEs), or special purpose vehicles

(SPVs)—to hold securitized [pooled] mortgages. Because the securitized mortgages were held by an off-balance sheet entity, however, the banks did not have to hold capital reserves against the risk of default—thus leaving them so vulnerable. Off-balance sheet operations are permitted by Financial Accounting Standards Board rules installed at the urging of big banks. The Securities Industry and Financial Markets Association and the American Securitization Forum are among the lobby interests now blocking efforts to get this rule reformed.

## Financial Derivatives

3. *The Executive Branch Rejects Financial Derivative Regulation.* Financial derivatives [securities with value derived from underlying assets] are unregulated. By all accounts this has been a disaster, as Warren Buffett's warning that they represent "weapons of mass financial destruction" has proven prescient. Financial derivatives have amplified the financial crisis far beyond the unavoidable troubles connected to the popping of the housing bubble.

The Commodity Futures Trading Commission (CFTC) has jurisdiction over futures, options and other derivatives connected to commodities [a basic good of commerce, e.g., gold]. During the [Bill] Clinton administration, the CFTC sought to exert regulatory control over financial derivatives. The agency was quashed by opposition from Treasury Secretary Robert Rubin and, above all, Fed [Federal Reserve] Chair Alan Greenspan. They challenged the agency's jurisdictional authority; and insisted that CFTC regulation might imperil existing financial activity that was already at considerable scale (though nowhere near present levels). Then Deputy Treasury Secretary Lawrence Summers told Congress that CFTC proposals "cas[t] a shadow of regulatory uncertainty over an otherwise thriving market."

4. *Congress Blocks Financial Derivative Regulation.* The deregulation—or nonregulation—of financial derivatives was

sealed in 2000, with the Commodity Futures Modernization Act (CFMA), passage of which was engineered by then Senator Phil Gramm, R-Texas. The Commodity Futures Modernization Act exempts financial derivatives, including credit default swaps, from regulation and helped create the current financial crisis.

---

*Enforcement activity would have protected homeowners, and lessened though not prevented the current financial crisis. But the regulators sat on their hands.*

---

## Bank Regulation

5. *The SEC's [Securities and Exchange Commission's] Voluntary Regulation Regime for Investment Banks.* In 1975, the SEC's trading and markets division promulgated a role requiring investment banks to maintain a debt-to-net-capital ratio of less than 12 to 1. It forbid trading in securities if the ratio reached or exceeded 12 to 1, so most companies maintained a ratio far below it. In 2004, however, the SEC succumbed to a push from the big investment banks—led by Goldman Sachs, and its then chair, Henry Paulson—and authorized investment banks to develop their own net capital requirements in accordance with standards published by the Basel Committee on Banking Supervision. This essentially involved complicated mathematical formulas that imposed no real limits, and was voluntarily administered. With this new freedom, investment banks pushed borrowing ratios to as high as 40 to 1, as in the case of Merrill Lynch. This super-leverage not only made the investment banks more vulnerable when the housing bubble popped, it enabled the banks to create a more tangled mess of derivative investments—so that their individual failures, or the potential of failure, became systemic crises. Former SEC chair Chris Cox has acknowledged that the voluntary regulation was a complete failure.

6. *Bank Self-Regulation Goes Global: Preparing to Repeat the Meltdown?* In 1988, global bank regulators adopted a set of rules known as Basel I, to impose a minimum global standard of capital adequacy for banks. Complicated financial maneuvering made it hard to determine compliance, however, which led to negotiations over a new set of regulations. Basel II, heavily influenced by the banks themselves, establishes varying capital reserve requirements, based on subjective factors of agency ratings and the banks' own internal risk-assessment models. The SEC experience with Basel II principles illustrates their fatal flaws. Commercial banks in the United States are supposed to be compliant with aspects of Basel II as of April 2008, but complications and intra-industry disputes have slowed implementation.

7. *Failure to Prevent Predatory Lending.* Even in a deregulated environment, the banking regulators retained authority to crack down on predatory lending abuses. Such enforcement activity would have protected homeowners, and lessened though not prevented the current financial crisis. But the regulators sat on their hands. The Federal Reserve took three formal actions against subprime lenders from 2002 to 2007. The Office of Comptroller of the Currency [OCC], which has authority over almost 1,800 banks, took three consumer-protection enforcement actions from 2004 to 2006.

8. *Federal Preemption of State Consumer Protection Laws.* When the states sought to fill the vacuum created by federal nonenforcement of consumer protection laws against predatory lenders, the feds jumped to stop them. "In 2003," as [former governor of New York] Eliot Spitzer recounted, "during the height of the predatory lending crisis, the Office of the Comptroller of the Currency invoked a clause from the 1863 National Bank Act to issue formal opinions preempting all state predatory lending laws, thereby rendering them inoperative. The OCC also promulgated new rules that prevented states from enforcing any of their own consumer protection laws against national banks."

## Subprime Loans

*9. Escaping Accountability: Assignee Liability.* Under existing federal law, with only limited exceptions, only the original mortgage lender is liable for any predatory and illegal features of a mortgage—even if the mortgage is transferred to another party. This arrangement effectively immunized acquirers of the mortgage ("assignees") for any problems with the initial loan, and relieved them of any duty to investigate the terms of the loan. Wall Street interests could purchase, bundle and securitize subprime loans [loans to borrowers with poor credit]—including many with pernicious, predatory terms—without fear of liability for illegal loan terms. The arrangement left victimized borrowers with no cause of action against any but the original lender, and typically with no defenses against being foreclosed upon. Representative Bob Ney, R-Ohio—a close friend of Wall Street who subsequently went to prison in connection with the [former lobbyist Jack] Abramoff scandal—was the leading opponent of a fair assignee liability regime.

*10. Fannie and Freddie Enter the Subprime Market.* At the peak of the housing boom, Fannie Mae [Federal National Mortgage Association] and Freddie Mac [Federal Home Loan Mortgage Corporation] were dominant purchasers in the subprime secondary market. The government-sponsored enterprises were followers, not leaders, but they did end up taking on substantial subprime assets—at least $57 billion. The purchase of subprime assets was a break from prior practice, justified by theories of expanded access to homeownership for low-income families and rationalized by mathematical models allegedly able to identify and assess risk to newer levels of precision. In fact, the motivation was the for-profit nature of the institutions and their particular executive incentive schemes. Massive lobbying—including especially but not only of Democratic friends of the institutions—enabled them to divert from their traditional exclusive focus on prime loans.

Fannie and Freddie are not responsible for the financial crisis. They are responsible for their own demise, and the resultant massive taxpayer liability.

---

*Congress must adopt the view that Wall Street has no legitimate seat at the table.*

---

## Lack of Federal Oversight

*11. Merger Mania.* The effective abandonment of antitrust and related regulatory principles over the last two decades has enabled a remarkable concentration in the banking sector, even in advance of recent moves to combine firms as a means to preserve the functioning of the financial system. The megabanks achieved too-big-to-fail status. While this should have meant they be treated as public utilities requiring heightened regulation and risk control, other deregulatory maneuvers (including repeal of Glass-Steagall) enabled these gigantic institutions to benefit from explicit and implicit federal guarantees, even as they pursued reckless high-risk investments.

*12. Rampant Conflicts of Interest: Credit Ratings Firms' Failure.* Credit ratings are a key link in the financial crisis story. With Wall Street combining mortgage loans into pools of securitized assets and then slicing them up into tranches [pieces], the resultant financial instruments were attractive to many buyers because they promised high returns. But pension funds and other investors could only enter the game if the securities were highly rated.

The credit rating firms enabled these investors to enter the game, by attaching high ratings to securities that actually were high risk—as subsequent events have revealed. The credit ratings firms have a bias to offering favorable ratings to new instruments because of their complex relationships with issuers and their desire to maintain and obtain other business dealings with issuers.

This institutional failure and conflict of interest might and should have been forestalled by the SEC, but the Credit Rating Agency Reform Act of 2006 gave the SEC insufficient oversight authority. In fact, the SEC must give an approval rating to credit ratings agencies if they are adhering to their own standards—even if the SEC knows those standards to be flawed.

## No Seat for Wall Street

Wall Street is presently humbled, but not prostrate. Despite siphoning trillions of dollars from the public purse, Wall Street executives continue to warn about the perils of restricting "financial innovation"—even though it was these very innovations that led to the crisis. And they are scheming to use the coming congressional focus on financial regulation to centralize authority with industry-friendly agencies.

If we are to see the meaningful regulation we need, Congress must adopt the view that Wall Street has no legitimate seat at the table. With Wall Street having destroyed the system that enriched its high flyers, and plunged the global economy into deep recession, it's time for Congress to tell Wall Street that its political investments have also gone bad. This time, legislating must be to control Wall Street, not further Wall Street's control.

# Government Policy, Not Lack of Regulation, Caused the Financial Crisis

*Peter J. Wallison*

*Peter J. Wallison is the Arthur F. Burns Fellow in Financial Policy Studies at the American Enterprise Institute for Public Policy Research and former general counsel of the U.S. Treasury Department.*

Two narratives seem to be forming to describe the underlying causes of the financial crisis. One, as outlined in a *New York Times* front-page story on Sunday, December 21 [2008], is that President [George W.] Bush excessively promoted growth in home ownership without sufficiently regulating the banks and other mortgage lenders that made the bad loans. The result was a banking system suffused with junk mortgages, the continuing losses on which are dragging down the banks and the economy. The other narrative is that government policy over many years—particularly the use of the Community Reinvestment Act and Fannie Mae [Federal National Mortgage Association] and Freddie Mac [Federal Home Mortgage Corporation] to distort the housing credit system—underlies the current crisis. The stakes in the competing narratives are high. The diagnosis determines the prescription. If the *Times* diagnosis prevails, the prescription is more regulation of the financial system; if instead government policy is to blame, the prescription is to terminate those government policies that distort mortgage lending.

There really isn't any question of which approach is factually correct: Right on the front page of the *Times* edition of December 21 is a chart that shows the growth of home own-

Peter J. Wallison, "The True Origins of This Financial Crisis: As Opposed to a Desperate Liberal Legend," *American Spectator*, vol. 42, February 2009, pp. 22–27. Copyright © The American Spectator 2009. Reproduced by permission.

ership in the United States since 1990. In 1993 it was 63 percent; by the end of the [Bill] Clinton administration it was 68 percent. The growth in the Bush administration was about 1 percent. The *Times* itself reported in 1999 that Fannie Mae and Freddie Mac were under pressure from the Clinton administration to increase lending to minorities and low-income home buyers—a policy that necessarily entailed higher risks. Can there really be a question, other than in the fevered imagination of the *Times*, where the push to reduce lending standards and boost home ownership came from?

The fact is that neither political party, and no administration, is blameless; the honest answer, as outlined below, is that government policy over many years caused this problem. The regulators, in both the Clinton and Bush administrations, were the enforcers of the reduced lending standards that were essential to the growth in home ownership and the housing bubble.

## Misguided Government Policy

There are two key examples of this misguided government policy. One is the Community Reinvestment Act (CRA). The other is the affordable housing "mission" that the government-sponsored enterprises (GSEs) Fannie Mae and Freddie Mac were charged with fulfilling.

---

*A law that was originally intended to encourage banks to use safe and sound practices in lending now required them to be "innovative" and "flexible."*

---

As originally enacted in 1977, the CRA vaguely mandated regulators to consider whether an insured bank was serving the needs of the "whole" community. For 16 years, the act was invoked rather infrequently, but 1993 marked a decisive turn in its enforcement. What changed? Substantial media and political attention was showered upon a 1992 Boston Federal Reserve Bank study of discrimination in home mortgage lending. This study concluded that, while there was no overt discrimination in banks' allocation of mortgage funds, loan officers gave whites preferential treatment. The methodology of the study has since been questioned, but at the time it was highly influential with regulators and members of the incoming Clinton administration; in 1993, bank regulators initiated a major effort to reform the CRA regulations.

In 1995, the regulators created new rules that sought to establish objective criteria for determining whether a bank was meeting CRA standards. Examiners no longer had the discretion they once had. For banks, simply proving that they were looking for qualified buyers wasn't enough. Banks now had to show that they had actually made a requisite number of loans to low- and moderate-income (LMI) borrowers. The new regulations also required the use of "innovative or flexible" lending practices to address credit needs of LMI borrowers and neighborhoods. Thus, a law that was originally intended to encourage banks to use safe and sound practices in lending now required them to be "innovative" and "flexible." In other words, it called for the relaxation of lending standards, and it was the bank regulators who were expected to enforce these relaxed standards.

## Looser Lending Standards

The effort to reduce mortgage lending standards was led by the Department of Housing and Urban Development through the 1994 National Homeownership Strategy, published at the request of President Clinton. Among other things, it called for "financing strategies, fueled by the creativity and resources of the private and public sectors, to help homeowners that lack cash to buy a home or to make the payments." Once the standards were relaxed for low-income borrowers, it would seem impossible to deny these benefits to the prime market. Indeed, bank regulators, who were in charge of enforcing CRA standards, could hardly disapprove of similar loans made to better-qualified borrowers.

---

*Fannie and Freddie used their affordable housing mission to avoid additional regulation by Congress.*

---

Sure enough, according to data published by the Joint Center for Housing Studies of Harvard University, from 2001 through 2006, the share of all mortgage originations that were made up of conventional mortgages (that is, the 30-year fixed-rate mortgage that had always been the mainstay of the U.S. mortgage market) fell from 57.1 percent in 2001 to 33.1 percent in the fourth quarter of 2006. Correspondingly, subprime loans (those made to borrowers with blemished credit) rose from 7.2 percent to 18.8 percent, and Alt-A loans (those made to speculative buyers or without the usual underwriting standards) rose from 2.5 percent to 13.9 percent. Although it is difficult to prove cause and effect, it is highly likely that the lower lending standards required by the CRA influenced what banks and other lenders were willing to offer to borrowers in prime markets. Needless to say, most borrowers would prefer a mortgage with a low down payment requirement, allowing them to buy a larger home for the same initial investment.

The problem is summed up succinctly by Stan Liebowitz of the University of Texas at Dallas:

> From the current handwringing, you'd think that the banks came up with the idea of looser underwriting standards on their own, with regulators just asleep on the job. In fact, it was the regulators who relaxed these standards—at the behest of community groups and "progressive" political forces. . . . For years, rising house prices hid the default problems since quick refinances were possible. But now that house prices have stopped rising, we can clearly see the damage done by relaxed loan standards.

The point here is not that low-income borrowers received mortgage loans that they could not afford. That is probably true to some extent but cannot account for the large number of subprime and Alt-A loans that currently [February 2009] pollute the banking system. It was the spreading of these looser standards to the prime loan market that vastly increased the availability of credit for mortgages, the speculation in housing, and ultimately the bubble in housing prices.

## Fannie's and Freddie's Junk Loans

In 1992, an affordable housing mission was added to the charters of Fannie and Freddie, which—like the CRA—permitted Congress to subsidize LMI housing without appropriating any funds. A 1997 Urban Institute report found that local and regional lenders seemed more willing than the GSEs to serve creditworthy low- to moderate-income and minority applicants. After this, Fannie and Freddie modified their automated underwriting systems to accept loans with characteristics that they had previously rejected. This opened the way for large numbers of nontraditional and subprime mortgages. These did not necessarily come from traditional banks, lending under the CRA, but from lenders like Countrywide Financial, the nation's largest subprime and nontraditional mortgage lender and a firm that would become infamous for consistently pushing the envelope on acceptable underwriting standards.

Fannie and Freddie used their affordable housing mission to avoid additional regulation by Congress, especially restrictions on the accumulation of mortgage portfolios (today totaling approximately $1.6 trillion) that accounted for most of their profits. The GSEs argued that if Congress constrained the size of their mortgage portfolios, they could not afford to adequately subsidize affordable housing. By 1997, Fannie was offering a 97 percent loan-to-value mortgage. By 2001, it was offering mortgages with no down payment at all. By 2007, Fannie and Freddie were required to show that 55 percent of their mortgage purchases were LMI loans and, within that goal, 38 percent of all purchases were to come from underserved areas (usually inner cities) and 25 percent were to be loans to low-income and very-low-income borrowers. Meeting these goals almost certainly required Fannie and Freddie to purchase loans with low down payments and other deficiencies that would mark them as subprime or Alt-A.

The decline in underwriting standards is clear in the financial disclosures of Fannie and Freddie. From 2005 to 2007, Fannie and Freddie bought approximately $1 trillion in subprime and Alt-A loans. This amounted to about 40 percent of their mortgage purchases during that period. Moreover, Freddie purchased an ever-increasing percentage of Alt-A and subprime loans for each year between 2004 and 2007. It is impossible to forecast the total losses the GSEs will realize from a $1.6 trillion portfolio of junk loans, but if default rates on these loans continue at the unprecedented levels they are showing today, the number will be staggering. The losses could make the $150 billion S&L [savings and loan association] bailout in the late 1980s and early 1990s look small by comparison.

*State-based residential finance laws give homeowners two free options that contributed substantially to the financial crisis.*

## The Effect on All Lenders

The GSEs' purchases of subprime and Alt-A loans affected the rest of the market for these mortgages in two ways. First, it increased the competition for these loans with private-label issuers. Before 2004, private-label issuers—generally investment and commercial banks—specialized in subprime and Alt-A loans because GSEs' financial advantages, especially their access to cheaper financing, enabled them to box private-label competition out of the conventional market. When the GSEs decided to ramp up their purchases of subprime and Alt-A loans to fulfill their affordable housing mission, they began to take market share from the private-label issuers while simultaneously creating greater demand for subprime and Alt-A loans among members of the originator community.

Second, the increased demand from the GSEs and the competition with private-label issuers drove up the value of subprime and Alt-A mortgages, reducing the risk premium that had previously suppressed originations. As a result, many more marginally qualified or unqualified applicants for mortgages were accepted. From 2003 to late 2006, conventional loans (including jumbo loans) declined from 78.8 percent to 50.1 percent of all mortgages, while subprime and Alt-A loans increased from 10.1 percent to 32.7 percent. Because GSE purchases are not included in these numbers, in the years just before the collapse of home prices began, about half of all home loans being made in the United States were non-prime loans. Since these mortgages aggregate more than $2 trillion, this accounts for the weakness in bank assets that is the principal underlying cause of the current financial crisis.

In a very real sense, the competition from Fannie and Freddie that began in late 2004 caused both the GSEs and the private-label issuers to scrape the bottom of the mortgage barrel. Fannie and Freddie did so in order to demonstrate to Congress their ability to increase support for affordable housing. The private-label issuers did so to maintain their market share against the GSEs' increased demand for subprime and Alt-A products. Thus, the gradual decline in lending standards—beginning with the revised CRA regulations in 1993 and continuing with the GSEs' attempts to show Congress that they were meeting their affordable housing mission—came to dominate mortgage lending in the United States.

## State Laws and Tax Laws

Federal housing initiatives are not the only culprits in the current mortgage mess—state-based residential finance laws give homeowners two free options that contributed substantially to the financial crisis. First, any homeowner may, without penalty, refinance a mortgage whenever interest rates fall or home prices rise to a point where there is significant equity in the home, enabling them to extract any equity that had accumulated between the original financing transaction and any subsequent refinancing. The result is so-called cash-out refinancing, in which homeowners treat their homes like savings accounts, drawing out funds to buy cars, boats, or second homes. By the end of 2006, 86 percent of all home mortgage refinancings were cash-outs, amounting to $327 billion that year. Unfortunately, this meant that when home prices fell, there was little equity in the home behind the mortgage and frequently little reason to continue making payments on the mortgage.

The willingness of homeowners to walk away from their "underwater" mortgages was increased by the designation of mortgages as "without recourse" in most states. In essence, non-recourse mortgages mean that defaulting homeowners are not personally responsible for paying any difference between the value of the home and the principal amount of the mortgage obligation, or that the process for enforcing this obligation is so burdensome and time-consuming that lenders simply do not bother. The homeowner's opportunity to walk away from a home that is no longer more valuable than the mortgage it carries exacerbates the effect of the cash-out refinancing.

Tax laws further amplified the problems of the housing bubble and diminished levels of home equity, especially the deductibility of interest on home equity loans. Interest on consumer loans of all kinds—for cars, credit cards, or other purposes—is not deductible for federal tax purposes, but interest on home equity loans is deductible no matter how the funds are used. As a result, homeowners are encouraged to take out home equity loans to pay off their credit card or auto loans or to make the purchases that would ordinarily be made with other forms of debt. Consequently, homeowners are encouraged not only to borrow against their homes' equity in preference to other forms of borrowing, but also to extract equity from their homes for personal and even business purposes. Again, the reduction in home equity has enhanced the likelihood that defaults and foreclosures will rise precipitously as the economy continues to contract.

## Bank Policies

Bank regulatory policies should also shoulder some of the blame for the financial crisis. Basel I, a 1988 international protocol developed by bank regulators in most of the world's developed countries, devised a system for ensuring that banks are adequately capitalized. Bank assets are assigned to different risk categories, and the amount of capital that a bank holds for each asset is pegged to the asset's perceived riskiness. Under Basel I's tiered risk-weighting system, AAA [high credit rating] asset-backed securities are less than half as risky as residential mortgages, which are themselves half as risky as commercial loans. These rules provided an incentive for banks to hold mortgages in preference to commercial loans or to convert their portfolios of whole mortgages into an MBS [mortgage-backed security] portfolio rated AAA, because doing so would substantially reduce their capital requirements.

Though the banks may have been adequately capitalized if the mortgages were of high quality or if the AAA rating correctly predicted the risk of default, the gradual decline in underwriting standards meant that the mortgages in any pool of prime mortgages often had high loan-to-value ratios, low FICO scores [developed by the Fair Isaac Corporation to measure credit risk], or other indicators of low quality. In other words, the Basel bank capital standards, applicable throughout the world's developed economies, encouraged commercial banks to hold only a small amount of capital against the risks associated with residential mortgages. As these risks increased because of the decline in lending standards and the ballooning of home prices, the Basel capital requirements became increasingly inadequate for the risks banks were assuming in holding both mortgages and MBS portfolios.

Preventing a recurrence of the financial crisis we face today does not require new regulation of the financial system. What is required instead is an appreciation of the fact—as much as lawmakers would like to avoid it—that U.S. housing policies are the root cause of the current financial crisis. Other players—greedy investment bankers; incompetent rating agencies; irresponsible housing speculators; shortsighted homeowners; and predatory mortgage brokers, lenders, and borrower—all played a part, but they were only following the economic incentives that government policy laid out for them. If we are really serious about preventing a recurrence of this crisis, rather than increasing the power of the government over the economy, our first order of business should be to correct the destructive housing policies of the U.S. government.

# Increasing Global Income Inequality Caused the Global Financial Crisis

*Branko Milanovic*

*Branko Milanovic is a lead economist in the World Bank's research department, where he works on the topics of income inequality and globalization. He is also an adjunct scholar with the Carnegie Endowment for International Peace. Milanovic is the author of* Worlds Apart: Measuring International and Global Inequality.

The current financial crisis is generally blamed on feckless bankers, financial deregulation, crony capitalism and the like. While all of these elements may be true, this purely financial explanation of the crisis overlooks its fundamental reasons. They lie in the real sector, and more exactly in the distribution of income across individuals and social classes. Deregulation, by helping irresponsible behavior, just exacerbated the crisis; it did not create it.

## Increased Income Inequality

To go to the origins of the crisis, one needs to go to rising income inequality within practically all countries in the world, and the United States in particular, over the last thirty years. In the United States, the top 1 percent of the population doubled its share in national income from around 8 percent in the mid-1970s to almost 16 percent in the early 2000s. That eerily replicated the situation that existed just prior to the crash of 1929, when the top 1 percent share reached its previous high-water mark. American income inequality over the

Branko Milanovic, "Two Views on the Cause of the Global Crisis—Part I," *YaleGlobal Online,* May 4, 2009. Copyright © 2009 Yale Center for the Study of Globalization. Reproduced by permission.

last hundred years thus basically charted a gigantic U, going down from its 1929 peak all the way to the late 1970s, and then rising again for thirty years.

What did the increase mean? Such enormous wealth could not be used for consumption only. There is a limit to the number of Dom Pérignons and Armani suits one can drink or wear. And, of course, it was not reasonable either to "invest" solely in conspicuous consumption when wealth could be further increased by judicious investment. So, a huge pool of available financial capital—the product of increased income inequality—went in search of profitable opportunities into which to invest.

---

*A way to make it seem that the middle class was earning more than it did was to increase its purchasing power through broader and more accessible credit.*

---

But the richest people and the hundreds of thousands somewhat less rich, could not invest the money themselves. They needed intermediaries, the financial sector. Overwhelmed with such an amount of funds, and short of good opportunities to invest the capital as well as enticed by large fees attending each transaction, the financial sector became more and more reckless, basically throwing money at anyone who would take it. While one cannot prove that investible resources eventually exceeded the number of safe and profitable investment opportunities (since nobody knows a priori [beforehand] how many and where there are good investment opportunities), this is strongly suggested by the increasing riskiness of investments that the financiers had to undertake.

## The Middle Class

But this is only one part of the equation: how and why large amounts of investable money went in search of a return on that money. The second part of the equation explains who borrowed that money. There again we go back to the rising inequality. The increased wealth at the top was combined with an absence of real economic growth in the middle. Real median wage in the United States has been stagnant for twenty-five years, despite an almost doubling of GDP [gross domestic product] per capita. About one-half of all real income gains between 1976 and 2006 accrued to the richest 5 percent of households. The new "gilded age" was understandably not very popular among the middle classes that saw their purchasing power not budge for years. Middle-class income stagnation became a recurrent theme in the American political life, and an insoluble political problem for both Democrats and Republicans. Politicians obviously had an interest to make their constituents happy for otherwise they may not vote for them. Yet they could not just raise their wages. A way to make it seem that the middle class was earning more than it did was to increase its purchasing power through broader and more accessible credit. People began to live by accumulating ever-rising debts on their credit cards, taking on more car debts or higher mortgages. President George W. Bush famously promised that every American family, implicitly regardless of its income, would be able to own a home. Thus was born the great American consumption binge which saw the household debt increase from 48 percent of GDP in the early 1980s to 100 percent of GDP before the crisis.

The interests of several large groups of people became closely aligned. High net-worth individuals and the financial sector were, as we have seen, keen to find new lending opportunities. Politicians were eager to "solve" the irritable problem of middle-class income stagnation. The middle class and those poorer than them were happy to see their tight budget constraint removed as if by a magic wand, consume all the fine things purchased by the rich, and partake in the longest US post–World War II economic expansion. Suddenly, the middle class too felt like the winners.

## An Unsustainable Binge

This is what more than two centuries ago, the great French philosopher Montesquieu mocked when he described the mechanism used by the creators of paper money in France (an experiment that eventually crumbled with a thud): "People of Baetica," wrote Montesquieu, "do you want to be rich? Imagine that I am very much so, and that you are very rich also; every morning tell yourself that your fortune has doubled during the night; and if you have creditors, go pay them with what you have imagined, and tell them to imagine it in their turn."

---

*The root cause of the crisis is not to be found in hedge funds and bankers who simply behaved with the greed to which they are accustomed.*

---

The credit-fueled system was further helped by the ability of the US to run large current account deficits; that is, to have several percentage points of its consumption financed by foreigners. The consumption binge also took the edge off class conflict and maintained the American dream of a rising tide that lifts all the boats. But it was not sustainable. Once the middle class began defaulting on its debts, it collapsed.

## The Real Cause of the Crisis

We should not focus on the superficial aspects of the crisis, on the arcane of how "derivatives" work. If "derivatives" they were, they were the "derivatives" of the model of growth pursued over the last quarter of a century. The root cause of the crisis is not to be found in hedge funds and bankers who simply behaved with the greed to which they are accustomed (and for which economists used to praise them). The real cause of the crisis lies in huge inequalities in income distribution that generated much larger investable funds than could be profitably employed. The political problem of insufficient economic growth of the middle class was then "solved" by opening the floodgates of the cheap credit. And the opening of the credit floodgates, to placate the middle class, was needed because in a democratic system, an excessively unequal model of development cannot coexist with political stability.

Could it have worked out differently? Yes, without thirty years of rising inequality, and with the same overall national income, income of the middle class would have been greater. People with middling incomes have many more priority needs to satisfy before they become preoccupied with the best investment opportunities for their excess money. Thus, the structure of consumption would have been different: Probably more money would have been spent on home-cooked meals than on restaurants, on near-home vacations than on exotic destinations, on kids' clothes than on designer apparel. More equitable development would have removed the need for the politicians to look around in order to fund palliatives with which to assuage the anger of the middle-class constituents. In other words, there would have been more equitable and stable development, which would have spared the United States, and increasingly the world, an unnecessary crisis.

# Trade Agreements Pushing Deregulation Caused the Financial Crisis

*Lori Wallach*

*Lori Wallach is director of the Global Trade Watch division of Public Citizen, a consumer advocacy organization that represents consumer interests in Congress.*

The devastation being caused by the global economic crisis to the lives and livelihoods of hundreds of millions of people around the world is not merely the result of bad practices by certain mega financial service firms, but the foreseeable outcome of one system of global economic governance—or more accurately anti-governance—that has been put into place and now must be replaced.

## The Impact of Trade Agreements

Over the last several decades, the U.S. foreign economic policy has been the implementation worldwide of a package of deregulation, liberalization, privatization, new property rights and new limits on government policy space, often dubbed the Washington Consensus or the neoliberal agenda. "Trade" agreements, such as those enforced by the World Trade Organization (WTO), and international agencies, such as the International Monetary Fund and the World Bank, have been the delivery mechanism for this radical global experiment. . . .

Few policy makers at home or abroad are aware of the myriad ways in which today's "trade" pacts constrain their policy space on various non-trade matters. In part, this is because of the relative "newness" of this backdoor channel for domestic deregulation. Prior to the establishment of the North American Free Trade Agreement (NAFTA) and the WTO in 1994 and WTO in 1995, the scope of trade agreements was limited to setting the terms of exchange of goods across borders, namely cutting tariffs and lifting quotas. Proponents of the new expansive model of international commercial agreements branded WTO and NAFTA as "trade agreements" and attacked as protectionist all those criticizing these pacts' overreach into non-trade matters. This rhetorical sleight of hand obscured the fact that these pacts were delivery mechanisms for a much broader economic package, of which trade liberalization per se is only one limited aspect.

And now we are living with the consequences of leaving our nation's economic well-being to be determined by private interests, who legally must focus on quarterly profit statements while operating under a system they helped devise that removes all obligations and responsibilities to the rest of us.

*Congress's stimulus spending of our tax dollars will not fully cycle through the U.S. economy, even though studies show that doing so provides important economic gains.*

Remedying the current crisis, avoiding future such crises and achieving economic justice and stability at home and abroad will require a new system of global economic governance that harnesses the benefits of trade while removing the many non-trade policy constraints that are obstacles to ensuring markets operate in a stable and productive manner.

This is a practical matter, not an ideological assertion.

For instance, the WTO's Financial Services Agreement [FSA] explicitly limits domestic regulation of banks, securities and insurance firms by the United States and over 100 other nations. While many in Congress fume about foreign banks, such as UBS [a financial services company in Switzerland], obtaining U.S. taxpayer bailout funds while simultaneously refusing to reveal information about possible tax evasion by its depositors, few realize that the WTO's FSA sets an array of limits on Congress's regulatory authority over foreign banks operating here. . . .

## Spending U.S. Tax Dollars

The WTO's procurement agreement and those of the FTAs [free trade agreements] into which the United States has entered limit how Congress may expend our tax dollars. Given the recent brouhaha attacking Buy American rules in the stimulus package as "protectionist," it is worth noting that the terms in question had nothing to do with tariffs or trade or the functioning of private markets. Rather at issue was Congress's right to decide how to best spend U.S. tax dollars in a manner that could stimulate our economy. Yet, "trade" pacts such as WTO and the FTAs set limits on Congress's decisions regarding use of our tax dollars in a manner that provides preferences for U.S.-made goods or U.S. firms.

Thus Congress's stimulus spending of our tax dollars will not fully cycle through the U.S. economy, even though studies show that doing so provides important economic gains. For instance, the $20 billion in funding for electronic medical record keeping in the 2009 economic recovery plan is probably more likely to be spent offshore rather than to employ Americans. Meanwhile, despite the hysteria regarding the Buy American rules relating to infrastructure projects, in reality even though the stimulus package included the much broader Senate version of Buy America rules, only a small share of that money can be directed into the U.S. economy thanks to the limits set in trade agreement procurement rules. For instance, firms operating in 39 countries, including all of Europe, that signed the highly controversial WTO procurement agreement and firms in the additional 13 countries who are signatories to U.S. FTAs must be treated as if they were U.S.

firms for certain aspects of even the covered spending. While there are some important exceptions listed in the U.S. schedule of commitments in these agreements that safeguard the right to use domestic preferences for some categories of goods, the United States altogether gave up its rights to provide preferences to U.S. firms regarding the construction and other service procurement contracts.

---

*The United States made its "trade" agreement commitments based on ideology rather than economic or other national interests.*

---

## Ideology over National Interest

That would be galling enough, but to make matters worse, the U.S. commitments to these constraints on domestic procurement policy demonstrate a consistent trend: The United States made its "trade" agreement commitments based on ideology rather than economic or other national interests. That is to say that U.S. officials were so intent on selling the expansive model delivered by the WTO and NAFTA to other countries— many of which were wisely opposed to such an overreach— that our commitments are much more expansive than other countries'. This sorry reality provides a different perspective on the hollering by Canada and the European Union (EU) against the stimulus bill's Buy American provisions. Both the EU and Canada wisely excluded considerably broader swaths of their procurement activity from WTO rules and, in the case of Canada, also from NAFTA. Because of this, the EU and Canada have no obligation to provide U.S. firms with access to a wide array of their government contracts. For instance, while the United States safeguards its preferences (only) for domestic iron and steel used in federally funded state transportation projects, Canada carved out steel, motor vehicles, and coal altogether (for all provinces, for all sectors), and also carved out all construction contracts issued by the Departments of Transport. The EU carved out of its WTO procurement obligations contracts awarded by federal governments and sub-federal governments in connection with activities in the areas of drinking water, energy, transport, or telecommunications.

The United States also made the broadest commitments to comply with the non-trade regulatory strictures of the WTO service-sector agreement regarding nonfinancial services. These broad obligations pose possible conflicts with President [Barack] Obama's health care, affordable pharmaceutical, and climate policies. The [Bill] Clinton administration signed up health insurance, pharmaceutical distribution and hospitals to conform with the strict policy constraints established by the WTO's General Agreement on Trade in Services (GATS). These rules simply ban certain commonly used policy tools even if applied to foreign firms on a nondiscriminatory basis.

Many of the specific proposals being discussed now in Congress and in legislatures in numerous countries to counter the current economic crisis and avoid future meltdowns violate the WTO's expansive constraints on *domestic* non-trade regulation. These are not "protectionist" measures, but rather are reasonable non-trade policies needed to address the crisis and rebuild the U.S. and world economies to promote productive, not speculative investment.

---

*Many policy makers and scholars have not come to terms with the systemic nature of the needed changes.*

---

## Cognitive Dissonance About Trade

For years, a brave few economists have reviewed the massive persistent U.S. trade deficits that have reached six percent of GDP [gross domestic product], warned that such imbalances were not sustainable and called for an array of urgent policy actions before a foreseeably devastating "market correction" occurred. Over the past 15 years of WTO and NAFTA, as 4.3 million U.S. manufacturing jobs were lost—1 in 4 of the entire sector—and U.S. real median wages sat at scarcely above 1973 levels, and income inequality rose to levels not seen since the robber baron era, those same economists and a growing number of policy makers warned about the hollowing out of the U.S. economy and the need for new policies. As the United States became a net importer of food and saw its total agriculture trade surplus plummet and overall our major exports shifted to raw materials rather than value-added goods, a growing number have come to question the global economic system that could result in such outcomes.

Yet, even as the evidence of systemic failure has become overwhelming with the current crisis thoroughly indicting the so-called neoliberal model that wrought these outcomes, a version of global cognitive dissonance seems to have taken hold. That is to say that, while the cries for reregulation are now issuing forth from many previously unimaginable quarters, many policy makers and scholars have not come to terms with the systemic nature of the needed changes. Thus, many very smart people are clinging to totally inconsistent views: For instance, we must dramatically reregulate finance to save the world, but we must also finish the WTO Doha [Development] Round (which would impose further financial deregulation) to save the world because "free trade" is good.

In part this situation is based on the lack of attention to the systemic manner in which the United States created the current model of economic non-governance. Many people seem to have started to believe the public relations mantra pitched by the beneficiaries of the status quo that the current system is inevitable or some force of nature. In fact, it is an intentional construct. In the 1970s, policy makers dismantled the Bretton Woods system, which was created after the Great Depression to govern capital-flow and exchange rate policy. Later, starting in the late 1980s, the deregulation drive involved the weakening and eventual repeal of the U.S. "New Deal" system of prudential and pro-consumer banking regulation. In an elegantly effective strategy, the same U.S. corporate interests, "free-market" think tanks and U.S. government officials behind this experiment exported this system of extreme financial service deregulation, constraints on an array of government regulatory policies and new rights and privileges for foreign investors and transnational firms through various international agencies and negotiations. They found a hospitable venue for this offensive in the obscure Uruguay Round negotiations of the General Agreement on Tariffs and Trade (GATT), which established the WTO.

## Trade Agreements About Non-Trade Issues

The WTO, and regional pacts such as NAFTA, the Central America Free Trade Agreement (CAFTA) and various other FTAs based on the NAFTA-CAFTA model exploded the past boundaries of trade agreements. Rather than focusing on traditional matters such as tariff cuts and opening quotas, these pacts require signatory countries to adopt an array of non-trade policies. These include limiting service-sector regulation including financial services, providing new foreign investor rights and privileges that incentivize and protect the relocation of production to low-wage venues, constraining domestic import safety and the inspection standards that may be applied, and even limiting how domestic tax dollars may be spent in procurement. Rather than trade agreements, these pacts were a global governance system that dramatically shifted the balance of power away from government oversight of the economy for the public interest.

For instance, the WTO enforces 17 agreements, only several of which have anything to do with trade per se, including the 1947 GATT, which until 1995 was the multilateral trade system. The WTO requires that "[e]ach Member shall ensure the conformity of its laws, regulations and administrative procedures with its obligations as provided in the annexed Agreements." Nations that fail to comply are subject to challenge in foreign tribunals, outside the jurisdiction and due process safeguards of domestic courts. These tribunals are empowered to authorize significant trade sanctions unless and until countries bring their laws into conformity with WTO constraints. The combination of overreaching, retrograde global rules constraining normal government regulatory activity and their strong enforcement, poses a very real threat. With nearly 150 WTO challenges to domestic law completed, the laws in question have been ruled against 90 percent of the time, and countries have repealed or altered their laws to comply. The only exception is the EU's refusal to remove its ban on beef treated with artificial growth hormones after being ordered to do so by the WTO. In order to maintain this policy, the EU has made an *annual* payment of the equivalent of $150 million in trade sanctions for the past decade. Given the record of WTO tribunals systematically ruling against domestic laws—many having nothing to do with trade—now the mere threat of a WTO challenge often suffices to derail a proposal before it is ever approved or implemented.

---

*Giant financial service firms . . . spent most of the 1990s pushing for an FSA that explicitly limited financial service regulation worldwide.*

---

## Financial Service Regulation

The conflict posed between global calls for reregulation and the WTO's existing financial service deregulation rules—and the additional deregulation on the Doha [Development] Round negotiating table—provides a stark example. Deregulation of the financial service sector—including banking, insurance, asset-management, pension-fund, securities, financial-information, and financial advisory services—has been among the most important, but least discussed, aspects of the WTO's agenda. Few researchers and policy makers now engaged in the debate about the crisis and its remedies are even aware of the WTO's Financial Services Agreement.

How did such expansive non-trade policy constraints end up in a "trade" agreement? The answer is that giant financial service firms—including some now receiving taxpayer bailout funds—spent most of the 1990s pushing for an FSA that explicitly limited financial service regulation worldwide. In effect, they locked in domestically and exported worldwide the extreme deregulation model that is a significant cause of the current crisis. This agreement was never even put to a vote in Congress. Rather, under the leadership of then Treasury Secretary Robert Rubin, the executive branch simply signed the pact and put it into effect.

In recent months, there has been an abundance of violations of the spirit, if not the letter, of the current globalization model and the agreements implementing it. Indeed, governments around the world have discussed—and in some cases, implemented—various measures to counter the crisis that contradict the fundamental precepts of the WTO and other trade pacts. A select few have noticed, as when a foreign bankers association insisted in late 2008 that the U.S. taxpayer funds committed to the "Troubled Asset Recovery Program" be available for them. But these outcries have been the exception: In the throes of the crisis, with more horrifying economic data emerging daily, the WTO incompatibility of domestic emergency measures has been a muted concern.

This situation will not last. While the outcomes of this model and public and government responses to the resulting crisis have led to press reports declaring the end of the neoliberal era, in fact the very policies that contributed to the crisis remain in place through the WTO, as do 100-plus countries' obligations to comply with them. As more detailed proposals emerge, the financial service firms who helped write the WTO rules will increasingly raise the trade-pact constraints to fight reregulation at the domestic and international levels. Policy makers and advocates must be ready with a meaningful and factually informed response and proposals to reform the countervailing WTO rules and avoid *further* expanding WTO financial service-sector deregulation through the current Doha [Development] Round agenda.

Current
**CONTROVERSIES**

# CHAPTER 2

# What Should Be Done About the Global Financial Crisis?

# Overview: Addressing the Global Financial Crisis

*World Economic Forum*

*The World Economic Forum is an independent international organization committed to improving the state of the world by engaging leaders in partnerships to shape global, regional, and industry agendas.*

When leaders of the G-20 countries—which combined account for almost 90% of world GDP [gross domestic product] and 80% of world trade—meet in London in April [2009], they will face a set of economic challenges unlike any encountered by global decision makers since the Great Depression. These include stabilizing a fragile financial system, stimulating demand at a time when interest rates are at or near zero in many countries, combating a dangerous turn towards protectionism and perhaps most importantly—taking the first steps towards redesigning the global governance structures that failed to prevent the crisis.

## Views on the Crisis

These same topics were the subject of extensive debate at this year's [2009 World Economic Forum] Annual Meeting, as participants sought to both formulate responses to the immediate crisis and develop a vision for the reforms that will inevitably follow it.

"We have two tasks: the first is to help manage the crisis and the second is to shape the post-crisis world," noted professor Klaus Schwab, founder and executive chairman of the World Economic Forum. "Because only if we look at longer term perspectives can we recreate trust in the economic system and in the future."

World Economic Forum Annual Meeting 2009, Cologny/Geneva: World Economic Forum, 2009. Reproduced by permission.

The short-term perspective is bleak, according to John Lipsky, first deputy managing director, International Monetary Fund (IMF), Washington, D.C. The IMF's latest forecast predicts global GDP growth will decelerate to a meagre 0.5% in 2009, the weakest showing since World War II. Global unemployment, meanwhile, is rising rapidly, with the bulk of layoffs still to come.

A protracted global slump, comparable to the Great Depression in duration, if not in depth, cannot be ruled out, some economists warned. "We cannot underestimate the challenges and the dangers we face in 2009," said Stephen S. Roach, chairman, Asia, Morgan Stanley, Hong Kong SAR [Special Administrative Region]. Badly over-leveraged [having high debt] US consumers are dramatically cutting back on spending, Roach noted, reversing one of the main sources of global demand during the previous boom.

---

*Actions taken by the G-20 governments must be coordinated to a far higher degree than they have been so far.*

---

## Views on the Causes of the Crisis

A number of sessions focused on the sources of the current crisis, with many participants, including Roach, arguing that they ultimately stem from the same global economic imbalances that have driven the large US and United Kingdom current account deficits and the similarly large surpluses of many exporting countries. Wen Jiabao, premier of the People's Republic of China, blamed "inappropriate macroeconomic policies of some economies and their unsustainable model of development." Vladimir Putin, prime minister of the Russian Federation, cited the harmful consequences of a global economy in which "one regional centre prints money without respite and consumes material wealth, while another regional centre manufactures inexpensive goods and saves money printed by other governments." However, Ferit Sahenk, chairman of Turkey's Dogus Group and Young Global Leader [of the World Economic Forum], expressed the views of many that "what is important is collective action" at this stage of the crisis.

If an extended slump is to be avoided through collective action, then G-20 leaders will need to act quickly on a number of fronts to restore business and consumer confidence, participants agreed. These include:

- Financial stabilization to repair bank balance sheets and revive lending

- Fiscal stimulus to boost aggregate demand

- Recapitalization of the IMF and other steps to restore capital flows to the developing countries

- Agreement on the outlines of a new system of global financial regulation

Above all, participants stressed, actions taken by the G-20 governments must be coordinated to a far higher degree than they have been so far. Otherwise, the risk of perverse and/or self-defeating consequences—such as continued market volatility—will remain high.

## Financial Stabilization

The threat of systemic collapse, which loomed last September [2008] following the failure of Lehman Brothers, has receded in the wake of public capital injections by the United States, the United Kingdom and other G-7 governments [Canada, France, Germany, Italy, and Japan], and liquidity interventions by the major central banks. However, bank balance sheets remain stuffed with non-performing loans and other "toxic" assets, deterring new lending. "In a deflationary environment, the weight of accumulating debt can sink the banking system and push the economy into depression" was the fear expressed by George Soros, chairman of Soros Fund Management, and shared by many participants.

Participants, however, differed on the best approach to fix the banking problem. Gordon Brown, United Kingdom prime minister and current chair of the G-20, suggested most of the group's leaders are leaning towards a "good bank/bad bank" model, in which governments either purchase impaired assets or offer guarantees to banks that keep them on their own balance sheets. "We need international discussion on what is the best model," he said. "But that appears to be the way forward."

However, this approach presents a number of practical problems: the chief one being how to price the purchased or guaranteed assets. Some participants warned that leaders risk undermining already weak public support for financial stabilization if they are seen as providing hidden subsidies to existing bank shareholders.

Given the staggering size of the liabilities—involved governments may end up impairing their own creditworthiness, warned Joseph E. Stiglitz, professor, Columbia University, USA. Nor is there any assurance banks will resume lending. "We may end up throwing more good money after bad," Stiglitz complained. Stiglitz and others argued that more should be done to rescue the system from the bottom up, by providing relief to homeowners faced with foreclosure.

---

*The world's leading central banks would appear to have almost exhausted their ability to spur an economic recovery.*

---

Most participants rejected the alternative of nationalizing troubled banks, predicting it would cause an exodus of private capital from the entire financial sector. "If governments wipe out private shareholders, I don't think private investors will ever invest in banks again. There would be no incentive," contended Tony Tan Keng Yam, deputy chairman and executive director, Government of Singapore Investment Corporation (GIC), Singapore.

## Fiscal Stimulus

With short-term interest rates effectively at zero in the United States and Japan, and further easing seen as imminent in the European Union [EU], the world's leading central banks would appear to have almost exhausted their ability to spur an economic recovery. Although some participants held out hope for "quantitative easing"—in which monetary authorities step up purchases of the risky assets of the private sector, most agreed coordinated fiscal stimulus in the G-20 countries is the best hope for supporting global demand. Justin Yifu Lin, the World Bank's chief economist, reminded participants that "the whole world is a closed economy," and that "fiscal stimuli will not work if they are not coordinated."

The scale and scope of various fiscal stimulus plans were highlighted throughout the Annual Meeting, but it was apparent . . . that the global coordination of these national plans was minimal. Taro Aso, prime minister of Japan, cited the stimulus package under consideration in Japan's parliament, the Diet, which includes fiscal measures equaling roughly 2% of the country's GDP. Wen Jiabao, premier of the People's Republic of China, told participants the two-year plan approved by his government would equal 16% of the country's GDP, and would be used to subsidize housing, railway construction and other infrastructure projects. The prospect for US President Obama's proposed stimulus package was also discussed.

Here, too, however, concerns were raised. Several participants questioned whether the packages announced to date are large enough to offset the decline in private investment and consumption. Others warned that financial markets might eventually rebel against increases in government borrowing, sending bond yields higher and negating much of the economic benefit.

Delays could also prove damaging, suggested Abhisit Vejja-jiva, prime minister of Thailand, citing his country's experience during the 1997–1998 Asian crisis. "If you act too late, you end up having to do it again and again," he said. "The political costs can become unsustainable, because the public begins to believe it is not worth it."

---

*Hopes to avoid an outright contraction in global output this year rest heavily on continued growth in the developing countries.*

---

President José Manuel Barroso of the European Commission signaled the need for coordinated action by the European Union's member states to address the crisis, noting that the EU collectively represents the largest economy in the world. He called for "a new triumph for coordinated European actions." Jean-Claude Trichet of the European Central Bank said the long-term objective should be to ensure the resilience of the global financial system. "We need to solve immediate problems as well as follow a sustainable recovery path, and ensure long-term stability."

## The Developing World

Hopes to avoid an outright contraction in global output this year rest heavily on continued growth in the developing countries. However, the financial crisis has resulted in an abrupt decline in capital flows to those countries, with the IMF estimating such flows will total just US$300 billion in 2009, half of last year's total. While nations with sizable international reserves, such as India and China, can compensate for this drought, at least for a time, developing debtor countries face severe constraints on their ability to combat recession.

The immediate, practical step the G-20 could take to address the problem, participants agreed, would be to increase the resources of the IMF and the other multilateral lending agencies, while giving them greater latitude to offer assistance to countries before they encounter balance-of-payments problems. "We need a crisis prevention capability, not just crisis resolution," Prime Minister Brown argued.

Prime Minister Aso noted that Japan has already offered the IMF a US$100 billion loan, while Lipsky said the fund hopes to obtain an additional US$150 billion from its other members. But even these amounts appear insufficient, argued Montek S. Ahluwalia, deputy chairman, Planning Commission, India. Ahluwalia called for a tripling of existing member quotas, as well as for more innovative steps, such as a generalized issue of Special Drawing Rights (SDRs). "We need to see some unique confidence-building measures," he said.

Multilateral financing will be of limited help if the private capital drain is not reversed, participants warned. Many cited an alarming rise in "financial protectionism" as a result of the crisis, with banks in the developed world redirecting funds to domestic lending, often at the behest of their governments.

## Reforming Financial Regulation

In an address to the Annual Meeting participants, German Chancellor Angela Merkel called for the adoption of a "new charter for a global economic order" based on sustainable economics. "This may even lead to a UN Economic Council, just as the [United Nations] Security Council was created after World War II," she said.

Participants generally viewed the case for regulatory reform as self-evident, given the excesses revealed by the crisis— although some in the financial industry cautioned against an overreaction that would further discourage lending and entrepreneurial risk taking.

When participants at an economic brainstorming session were polled on the issue the G-20 should make its single highest priority, 40.6% listed the lack of an international regulatory framework, while 21.3% cited the absence of effective oversight of the use of financial leverage.

Above all, participants agreed, regulators need to ensure greater market transparency, both through closer surveillance and by facilitating the shift of over-the-counter derivatives trading to regulated exchanges. Bank capital standards ... will also need to be reviewed, and the internal risk models used by banks to implement those standards must be completely overhauled. Likewise, the role of the credit rating agencies in assigning risk levels (and thus the required capital backing) to assets is in question.

Participants rejected as unrealistic the idea of a single, supranational regulatory authority, concluding that informal bodies such as the Financial Stability Forum, which draws together prudential regulators and monetary policy makers, will have to provide the closer coordination the system desperately needs.

A number of participants suggested this collaboration should include the development of anti-cyclical regulatory policies—such as capital requirements and leverage restrictions that can be tightened during booms and loosened during downturns. Industry participants, however, were sceptical. "Political pressures will prevent it from working," predicted Walter B. Kielholz, chairman of the board of directors of Credit Suisse.

With the economic downturn still deepening, the need for a rapid, effective and coordinated response to the crisis naturally dominated the economic agenda at this year's Annual Meeting.

However, participants also stressed that the G-20 governments, as well as other global decision makers, can ill afford to ignore the world's longer term challenges, such as reducing poverty, controlling the spread of infectious diseases, arresting global climate change and—not least—correcting the structural imbalances in global savings and consumption that contributed to the crisis.

"What we are experiencing," Schwab reminded participants, "is the birth of a new era, a wake-up call to overhaul our institutions, our systems and, above all, our way of thinking."

# Temporary Nationalization of Banks Is Necessary

*Matthew Rothschild*

*Matthew Rothschild is the editor of the* Progressive, *a monthly political magazine committed to nonviolence and freedom of speech.*

One Treasury official after another is doing somersaults on a wire to distract us from the obvious: We need to nationalize many of the banks, not save them as private entities.

## Indefinite Bailouts

The banks got us into this financial mess in the first place by making unwise home loans and by speculating in unregulated credit default swaps [a type of financial instrument] tied to those loans. They have taken the entire world economy down with them. They don't deserve to be bailed out.

If our government really believed in free enterprise, these banks would be out of business right now.

Instead, first the Bush administration and now the Obama administration have decided to act like an iron lung for the banks, pumping hundreds of billions of dollars into them to keep them alive.

There is no reason to do that.

And it would have been cheaper to buy them outright.

"The day we gave Citigroup their second infusion we could have bought them for the same $20 billion," says economist Dean Baker. "On top of that, we guaranteed $300 billion of assets. We could have bought Citigroup several times over."

Still, the banks aren't solvent. Baker estimates that the losses on most of their balance sheets outweigh their capital. This is a recipe for indefinite bailouts.

Matthew Rothschild, "Nationalize the Banks," *Progressive*, vol. 73, no. 3, March 2009, pp. 8–9. Copyright © 2009 by The Progressive, Inc. Reproduced by permission of The Progressive, 409 East Main Street, Madison, WI 53703, www.progressive.org.

## Banks Are Not Lending

Nobel Prize winner in economics Joseph [E.] Stiglitz also sees the irrationality of leaving the banks in private hands.

"In effect, the American taxpayers are the major provider of finance to the banks," he wrote on CNN's Web site. "In some cases, the value of our equity injection, guarantees, and other forms of assistance dwarfs the value of the 'private' sector's equity contribution. Yet we have no voice in how the banks are run."

We don't have a voice because the Bush administration tied no strings to the $350 billion. But if we're the major shareholders, as we now are with Citigroup (taxpayers hold a 7.8 percent stake) and Bank of America (6 percent), we ought to have a major say. And if we're going to throw more money at them, why not just purchase the banks themselves?

The banks have not done what the government told us they were supposed to do when it lavished the first $350 billion on them. They didn't start lending more.

"The last thing in their minds was to restart lending," wrote Stiglitz. And even today, they have a strong incentive to sit on their cash.

---

*Truly nationalized banks, run by the government for the people, would help out the economy as a whole.*

---

"There is still no assurance of a resumption of lending," Stiglitz explains. "Having been burned once, many bankers are staying away from the fire. . . . Many a bank may decide that the better strategy is a conservative one: Hoard one's cash, wait until things settle down, hope that you are among the few surviving banks, and then start lending. Of course, if all the banks reason so, the recession will be longer and deeper than it otherwise would be."

## Social Returns from Nationalization

So, since lending is vital to the economy, and since the private banks won't lend, let's buy up some insolvent banks so we can get the lending going ourselves. The private sector has proven that it can't or won't do the job. The public sector must step in. Put a different way, if we want companies to receive loans, why not get rid of the middleman, and have the government lend directly to businesses and to homeowners?

"For the moment, there's no choice," says Robert Pollin, professor of economics at the University of Massachusetts-Amherst. "Relative to a year ago, lending in the U.S. economy is down an astonishing 90 percent. The government needs to take over the banks now, and force them to start lending." (Pollin wants the government to sell the banks back into private hands, later on, with stringent regulations.)

---

*Keeping the banks in private hands isn't getting the job done.*

---

Truly nationalized banks, run by the government for the people, would help out the economy as a whole. As Stiglitz put it, under private ownership, there's a "huge gap between private rewards and social returns." Under public ownership, "the incentives of the banks can be aligned better with those of the country. And it is in the national interest that prudent lending be restarted."

We could reap other social returns from nationalization, as well. "If the banks were nationalized, the government could declare a moratorium on foreclosures for the properties it controls, and move to restructure mortgages—perhaps at subsidized rates—for homeowners," writes Joshua Holland of AlterNet.org.

## Money for Nothing

As it is right now, we're getting some of the vices of nationalization without all the virtues. We're shelling out gobs of public money for these companies—in many cases, more money than the companies are actually worth—but we're not running these companies in the public interest. We're allowing the companies to remain in private hands, for private purposes.

"We have a financial system that is run by private shareholders, managed by private institutions, and we'd like to do our best to preserve that system," said Treasury Secretary Timothy Geithner.

Why is that the job of the Obama administration?

I thought its job was to make the economy work for the American public. And keeping the banks in private hands isn't getting the job done. Throwing hundreds of billions of dollars, over and over, to keep these banks on life support makes no sense.

Unless you want to ensure that the shareholders get artificially inflated returns and the executives get to keep their jobs.

Or unless you are too snug in your ideological straitjacket to even consider the most rational way to proceed.

And that's the problem today. The word "nationalization" shuts off the debate. Never mind that Britain, facing the same crisis we are, just nationalized the Bank of Scotland. Never mind that Ronald Reagan himself considered such an option during a global banking crisis in the early 1980s.

"When a bank is insolvent, the regulators put it into receivership," says James Galbraith, professor of government at the LBJ School of Public Affairs of the University of Texas at Austin. "The Reagan administration had a plan to do it with all the big banks in 1982 and 1983, if a single large Latin American country had defaulted. Let me repeat that: the Reagan administration."

But the Obama administration is not considering receivership, much less genuine nationalization in the interests of the majority of Americans. Cluttered with worshippers of the private sector, skittish about being tagged "leftist," and beset by obdurate Republicans, the Obama administration has blocked off the path to true nationalization. Instead, it is opting for gimmicky proposals to take some bad debts off the books—all in service of those "private shareholders" that Geithner so adores.

## The Private Sector

Granted, nationalization over the long haul is a risky business, too, which is why Pollin resists it.

"We would have every reason to expect a wide range of failures and misjudgments, including 'crony capitalism'— privileged backroom dealings with selected nonfinancial firms," Pollin writes in *Boston Review*.

Pollin is also worried about the political fallout. "The failures of the nationalized system could be the very thing— perhaps the only thing—that could shift the target of public outrage over the collapse of the financial system off Wall Street and onto the U.S. government," he wrote.

While these are certainly legitimate concerns, we've seen what the private sector does—not only when left to its own devices but also when bailed out by hundreds of billions of our funds.

Yes, if it took over some of the banks, the government would have to carefully design a system to prevent corruption. And yes, there would be bumps along the road.

But we've had enough bumps on the road marked "private."

If we're going to be shelling out the money, we might as well run the store.

# Banks Should Not Be Nationalized

*Deroy Murdock*

*Deroy Murdock is a syndicated columnist with the Scripps Howard News Service and a contributing editor at National Review Online.*

L ast Labor Day [2008], the thought of nationalizing banks was alien, if not seditious. Today [February 20, 2009], some argue for bank expropriation. Bafflingly, this advice comes not from Communists, but from Republicans.

## The Call for Nationalization

"It may be necessary to temporarily nationalize some banks in order to facilitate a swift and orderly restructuring," former Federal Reserve chairman Alan Greenspan said in Wednesday's *Financial Times* [*FT*]. This would "allow the government to transfer toxic assets to a bad bank without the problem of how to price them." Greenspan, whose monetary bubble elevated the economy to the vertiginous heights from which it is tumbling, seems old enough to understand that banking without the "problem" of prices is like flying without the "problem" of altimeters.

Why do newspapers still seek this man's counsel?

For Sen. Lindsey Graham (R-SC), mere practicality trumps free-market principle. "We should be focusing on what works," Graham chirped to the *FT*. "If nationalization is what works, then we should do it." Graham claimed that many GOP senators—including former Republican presidential nominee John McCain—want nationalization "on the table."

The idea of government commandeering banks is nothing new. It appeared in 1848 in *The Communist Manifesto.*

"The proletariat will use its political supremacy, to wrest, by degrees, all capital from the bourgeoisie," Karl Marx predicted. This would include "centralization of credit in the hands of the State, by means of a national bank with State capital and an exclusive monopoly."

While Marx's proposal exceeded the ambitions of Greenspan, Graham, and Graham's GOP pals, it took liberal Democrats to declare bank nationalization out of bounds.

---

*Why not try something that actually would stimulate rather than enslave banks?*

---

"We have a financial system that is run by private shareholders, managed by private institutions, and we'd like to do our best to preserve that system" said Treasury Secretary Timothy Geithner.

"I would not be for nationalizing," said Sen. Charles Schumer (D-NY) as he moved to the right of these Republicans. "I think government's not good at making these decisions as to who gets loans and how this happens."

## Ideas from the Right

Rather than parrot Karl Marx, Greenspan, Graham, and other Republicans who have wandered off the ranch, Republicans should offer radical ideas—from the right. Why not help this wobbly industry by declaring a five-year federal tax holiday on banks? Let bankers improve their bottom lines and lend to worthy borrowers without worrying about the 35-percent corporate tax. Would that cost the Treasury tax revenue? Yes, but since Washington no longer checks price tags, why not try something that actually would stimulate rather than enslave banks? Improved economic growth and consequent decreases in government assistance could make this policy revenue positive.

Also, economist Allen Sinai estimates that some $1 trillion languishes offshore, enervated by America's high corporate and personal income taxes. Why not welcome this capital home until December 31—tax free, no penalties, no questions asked? It will create more jobs here than in Zurich.

The Senate on February 3 defeated an amendment by John Ensign (R-NV) and Barbara Boxer (D-CA) that would have allowed this money to be repatriated at a very attractive 5.25 percent tax rate. Of the $1 trillion out there, Sinai forecasts that $545 billion would return to America. That sum is equal to nearly 70 percent of the $787-billion spending bill that President Obama signed Tuesday. Surely, $545 billion would boost growth and employment.

In their book, *Global Tax Revolution*, the Cato Institute's Chris Edwards and Dan Mitchell report that a 2004 repatriation program targeted the $800 billion in U.S. assets then afloat overseas. That year, some $300 billion flowed back into the United States. "Intel Corporation repatriated $6 billion," they wrote, "which helped it finance construction of a new facility in Arizona."

Mitchell notes the paradox in how Uncle Sam handles the money of non-Americans versus Americans. "Foreigners get tax-haven treatment for investing in the U.S.," Mitchell says, "while U.S. citizens get hit over the head with double and triple taxation no matter where they invest."

How did America sink so low as to witness Republican calls for bank confiscation?

## The Emergence of Nationalization

As late as last summer, this economy was a virgin to nationalization. One of the most repugnant facets of former president Bush's malodorous legacy is that he stole America's chastity on nationalization. Bush used taxpayer dollars to buy 79.9 percent of insurer AIG. He fully absorbed Fannie Mae [Federal National Mortgage Association] and Freddie Mac [Federal Home Mortgage Corporation] into the state. The GM and Chrysler bailout—killed by the Senate, but autocratically imposed by Bush anyway—is turning these auto companies into *de facto* federal agencies. Rather than the Car Czar that Bush envisioned, an Obama-appointed automotive politburo will steer GM and Chrysler into the sunset.

Regarding nationalization, America's free market has devolved in half a year from unsullied maiden to street-corner whore. This sad truth is one more reason for the American Right to repudiate the Bush-Rove-Paulson borrow-spend-and-bailout model and its architects, as if severing and discarding an infected appendix.

That prominent Republicans must be reminded of these fundamentals confirms just how grim things have grown. As the song says: Breathe deep the gathering gloom.

# A Global Policy Response Is Necessary to Address the Global Financial Crisis

## C. Fred Bergsten

*C. Fred Bergsten is director of the Peterson Institute for International Economics, a nonpartisan research institution devoted to the study of international economic policy.*

The financial and economic crisis is a global phenomenon. No country has been spared. The downturn has been, and continues to be, rapidly transmitted across borders through both trade and financial channels.

## A Global Policy Package

A global policy response is therefore imperative. Unfortunately, the reactions to date have been limited to individual national efforts. Some countries, like China and the United States, have adopted sizable fiscal and monetary stimulus programs that will be extremely helpful. Others, including most of Europe and some of the emerging-market economies, have done relatively little. My colleague Simon Johnson has analyzed the causes of the crisis and presented a pessimistic forecast of the outlook in the absence of major new policy measures, and I will suggest what those measures should be.

The upcoming G-20 summit in London on April 2 [2009] offers the best (and perhaps last) opportunity to launch the needed global policy package. The G-20 countries account for about 80 percent of the world economy and could thus have a decisive impact. The summit will be the first multilateral meet-

C. Fred Bergsten, "Testimony to the House Committee on Foreign Affairs, Subcommittee on Terrorism, Nonproliferation, and Trade, Hearing on U.S. Foreign Economic Policy in the Global Crisis," *Peterson Institute for International Economics*, March 12, 2009. Copyright © 2009 Peter G. Peterson Institute for International Economics. Reproduced by permission of the author.

ing for President [Barack] Obama, appropriately so in light of the gravity of the economic situation and the priority that he has rightly accorded these issues in the early days of his administration.

---

*Ambitious new government stimulus will be the only way to restore adequate growth of demand in the world economy for the foreseeable future.*

---

The G-20 should adopt a four-part policy package to arrest the continuing decline of world output and promote recovery over the course of 2009 and into 2010:

- Major fiscal stimulus by virtually all member countries;

- A comprehensive political commitment to avoid all new protectionist trade distortions;

- Mobilization of large amounts of capital to support beleaguered developing countries, mainly through the International Monetary Fund;

- And initial steps toward reform of financial regulation to reduce the risk of future crises.

## Fiscal Stimulus

With private financial markets still largely frozen and consumer confidence at record lows, ambitious new government stimulus will be the only way to restore adequate growth of demand in the world economy for the foreseeable future. Much of this stimulus must be provided by central banks, along with the essential supports for the financial systems themselves, through both injections of massive amounts of liquidity and easing of monetary policies. Fortunately, most central banks have now moved decisively in this direction. In any event, most of the G-20 central banks are independent of their governments; they are thus not participating in the London summit nor would it be propitious for the governments to address the monetary issues overtly and publicly.

This requires governments to use fiscal initiatives to make their needed contribution to recovery. To date, the G-20 countries have adopted stimulus programs amounting to 1.4–1.7 percent of their aggregate GDP [gross domestic product]. No more than half a dozen of them have adopted expansions equaling 2 percent of their economies, which has been the notional international target advanced by the International Monetary Fund (IMF) and others to this point. The IMF estimates that the real economic impact of the measures to date will be under 1 percent of global output in 2009 and only a few tenths of 1 percent in 2010.

In light of the rapid deterioration of the growth outlook, the G-20 in London should adopt more ambitious fiscal stimulus targets of 3 percent of their economies for each of the next two years. This would inject total new demand of perhaps $1–1.5 trillion into the world economy in both 2009 and 2010. Countries that can and should do more clearly include Brazil, Canada, France, Germany, Korea, and Mexico.

## Global Coordination

There are at least four reasons why the fiscal stimulus program should be coordinated globally. First, it will probably be much too small unless all major countries contribute to it. Second, it would then be unbalanced geographically and lead to a renewal (or even further increase) in the global imbalances (US deficit, Chinese and Japanese surpluses) that helped bring on the crisis in the first place. Third, "free riding" by nonparticipants will be widely perceived elsewhere as unfair and add to the risk of protectionist trade reactions. Fourth, and perhaps most important, widespread participation will reduce the risk that any individual country will be penalized by the markets for adding temporarily to its fiscal deficit.

Each country would decide how to shape the details of its fiscal package. "Credit" would be given for programs that were already launched in response to the crisis, such as the recent $787 billion legislation in the United States and the $586 billion effort in China. A couple of the financially more precarious G-20 countries, such as Turkey and perhaps Italy, might be excused from the commitment because of the fragility of their budget positions and shaky credit ratings.

The key conceptual issue is to view each of the national stimulus programs as part of a comprehensive global strategy. In light of the intimate trade and financial linkages among virtually all countries that have now been so clearly revealed, including all the G-20 countries, it is essential to spur global demand if any individual nation is to experience an early turnaround. One of the key lessons from the Great Depression is that worldwide expansion policies were a key factor in generating recovery and growth across a wide range of countries in the 1930s.

---

*The fundamental reason for avoiding protectionism . . . is that the basic objective is to enhance global demand.*

---

## Avoiding Protectionism

It is also imperative that the G-20 countries adopt a firm political commitment to avoid adoption of any additional measures that would distort international trade and financial flows. Their pledge to do so at their previous summit on November 15 [2008] has already been violated by at least seventeen members of the group (excepting only Japan, Mexico, and Saudi Arabia). This has already led to emulation and retaliation by trading partners. The obvious risk is that world trade, which is declining for the first time in over 25 years, will fall sharply and produce a downward spiral of global growth as it did in the 1930s.

It will not be good enough for the G-20 to reiterate their fealty to their international legal commitments. The rules of the World Trade Organization (WTO) are exceedingly porous and "legal protectionism" is just as dangerous as any other kind. Moreover, there are no rules to effectively cover international investment. The London pledges must be comprehensive. . . .

The global nature of the problem is again paramount. The fundamental reason for avoiding protectionism, including in domestic stimulus programs like the recent US fiscal package and in the use of financial rescue funds, is that the basic objective is to enhance global demand. Buy-national restrictions, or lend-national requirements, obviously subvert that goal and must therefore be avoided.

The United States has a particular interest in this part of the package. Rapid export growth and sizable reductions in our trade deficit, which has fallen by about half from its peak in 2006, kept the US economy growing for a full year, from late 2007 through the third quarter of 2008, even though domestic demand was already declining due to the onset of the financial crisis. With the renewed strengthening of the dollar, we should in particular be expanding the activities of our export support programs (especially the Export-Import Bank) and pursuing trade policies that seek to further open markets around the world.

## Mobilizing Resources for Developing Countries

Developing countries now make up roughly half the global economy. Hence their ability to recover will have a major impact on our own prospects and those of the entire world. The developing countries actually held up remarkably well through the third quarter of last year, lending credence to the "decoupling" concept and even the "reverse coupling" idea that they could sustain the world as a whole. Led by China and India, they are still doing much better as a group than the industrialized countries but many of them have also fallen off a cliff over the past six months.

Any effective global recovery strategy must therefore accord a central role to this group of nations. In addition to rapidly shrinking markets for their exports, they have experienced a huge cutback in private capital inflows. They need offsetting support from public investment, which only the International Monetary Fund can provide in sizable amounts on short notice.

The G-20 should thus direct the IMF to undertake three major new programs. First, it should inject liquidity with little or no conditionality to developing countries that have suffered sharp declines in exports or capital inflows due to the global slowdown rather than any policy errors of their own. This could require as much as $500 billion of additional resources for the Fund, which should mainly be provided by the large surplus countries with excessive foreign exchange reserves (notably China, the major oil exporters, and Japan, which has already offered to contribute $100 billion).

Second, it should resume creating Special Drawing Rights (SDRs), which the IMF inaugurated in the late 1960s, to deal with reserve shortfalls of precisely the type feared by many developing countries today. An early creation of $250 billion, which could be supported by the United States without new legislation, would ease the financial anxieties afflicting numerous countries and obviate the need for "new mercantilist" measures to build reserves by running large trade surpluses instead. If the crisis and "new mercantilism" pressures persist, a second and larger SDR allocation could be added later.

Third, the Fund should substantially increase its regular quotas to enable it to conduct its traditional, conditional lending programs on the much larger scale required by the current crisis. This would also provide an opportunity, which the richer countries must seize if the emerging markets are to accept the standstill on trade barriers and new IMF-WTO mechanism on currency manipulation described above, to substantially alter the governance structure of both the Fund and the World Bank by providing much larger shares for the newly important emerging markets. The European Union and the United States should also take the occasion to give up their anachronistic holds on the top positions at the IMF and World Bank, respectively, and substitute a merit-based selection system instead. This "grand bargain" has been espoused by Prime Minister Gordon Brown of the United Kingdom, who will chair the London summit, and should be strongly supported by the United States.

---

*The current need is to promote renewed lending by financial institutions, on as large a scale as possible.*

---

## Financial Regulatory Reform

Some G-20 leaders have attempted to focus the meetings of the group, both last November and upcoming next month [April 2009], on reform of financial regulation at both the national and international levels. Such a view is fully understandable in light of the substantial contribution of inadequate regulation to bringing on the crisis. Reform is clearly needed to prevent a repetition of the current tragedy.

Such reform is a long-term rather than immediate project, however. This is partly because of the complexity of the issues and the consequent difficulty of addressing them quickly. But it is also because the current need is to promote renewed lending by financial institutions, on as large a scale as possible, and new steps to restrain that lending for prudential reasons would send mixed signals that could derail the recovery strategy. Most important, addressing this set of issues would divert attention from the overriding priority of promoting renewed growth. The G-20 in London should thus continue the process of moving toward reform that they began in Washington, and perhaps provide a bit more guidance to it, but spend most of their time on the first three issues outlined above.

# The United States Must Lead the Way in Restoring the Global Economic System

*Martin Wolf*

*Martin Wolf is associate editor and chief economics commentator at the* Financial Times, London. *He is the author of* Fixing Global Finance.

We are experiencing the most dangerous financial and economic crisis since the 1930s. But it is also a crisis for foreign policy: A deep recession will shake political stability across the globe; and it threatens the long-standing US goal of an open and dynamic global economy. Perhaps most important, the US is currently seen as the source of the problem rather than of the solution.

This crisis is, therefore, a devastating blow to US credibility and legitimacy across the world. If the US cannot manage free market capitalism, who can? If free market capitalism can bring such damage, why adopt it? If openness to the world economy brings such dangers, why risk it? As the shock turns to anger, not just in the US, but across the world, these questions are being asked. If the US wishes to obtain the right answers, it must address the crisis at home, and do what it can to rescue innocent victims abroad. This is not a matter of charity. It is a matter of enlightened self-interest.

## A Severe Crisis

The global economic crisis has become extremely severe: The financial system is on life support, with trillions of dollars of support by governments; three of the world's four most im-

Martin Wolf, "Testimony Before the Senate Foreign Relations Committee, Hearing on Foreign Policy and the Global Financial Crisis," Foreign.Senate.gov, March 25, 2009. Reproduced by permission of the author.

portant central banks—the Federal Reserve [the Fed], the Bank of Japan and the Bank of England—have interest rates at close to zero, with the European Central Bank likely to follow; governments are also loosening fiscal policy aggressively, with the deficits of advanced countries that are members of the G-20 forecast at 6.7 per cent of GDP [gross domestic product] this year [2009] and 7.6 per cent in 2010.

This massive policy support comes in response to increasingly dire economic conditions: The International Monetary Fund forecasts that global output will shrink by between 0.5 per cent and 1 per cent this year, a downgrade of 1 to 1.5 percentage points in two months; it also forecasts that the economies of advanced countries will shrink by between 3 and 3.5 per cent, the worst performance since the 1930s.

---

*All emerging economies are adversely affected by the loss of external demand, the shrinkage in global capital flows and the associated jumps in the price of borrowing.*

---

## Affected Countries

None of this is surprising. Not only did the global financial system seize up at the end of last year [2008], but the Asian Development Bank has reported that the total loss of worldwide market wealth is $50 trillion, close to a year's world output. The loss of stock market wealth alone is $25 trillion. Demand for manufactures, world manufactured output and world trade in manufactures fell off a cliff at the end of last year: Germany's industrial output was down 19.2 per cent year-on-year in January, South Korea's down 25.6 per cent and Japan's down 30.8 per cent.

Inevitably, and tragically, the most adversely affected are countries that have opened themselves up to global capital flows, particularly emerging countries in central and Eastern Europe. These were the only significant group of emerging economies to be net importers of capital in the 2000s, with results often seen before over the past three decades when capital takes flight. These countries face the risk of a melt-down, precisely because they trusted both Europe and the capital markets. The consensus of forecasts for growth of Eastern Europe this year has fallen from 6 per cent to minus 0.5 per cent since last June. It will surely fall far further. But all emerging economies are adversely affected by the loss of external demand, the shrinkage in global capital flows and the associated jumps in the price of borrowing.

## Change to the World

In a recent article for the *Financial Times*, which launched our series on the "Future of Capitalism", I argued that it is impossible to know where we are going. In the chaotic 1970s, few guessed that the next epoch would see the taming of inflation, the unleashing of capitalism and the death of communism. What will happen now depends on choices unmade and shocks unknown.

---

*The more imaginative and energetic the US now is, the better able it will be to restore its reputation and influence across the globe.*

---

Yet the combination of a financial collapse with a huge recession will surely change the world. The Great Depression transformed capitalism and the role of government for half a century. It led to the collapse of liberal trade, fortified the credibility of socialism and communism and shifted many policy makers towards import substitution as a development strategy. It led to xenophobia and authoritarianism. The search for security will strengthen political control over markets. A shift towards politics also entails a shift towards the national, away from the global. This is already evident in finance. But protectionist intervention is likely to extend well beyond the cases seen so far: These are still early days.

In emerging countries, the number of people in extreme poverty will rise, the size of the new middle class will fall and governments of some countries will default. Confidence in local and global elites, in the market and even in the possibility of material progress will weaken, with potentially devastating social and political consequences.

The ability of the West in general and the US in particular to influence the course of events will also be damaged. The collapse of the Western financial system, while China's apparently flourishes, marks a humiliating end to the "unipolar moment". As Western policy makers struggle, their credibility lies broken.

These changes will endanger the ability of the world not just to manage the global economy but also to cope with strategic challenges: fragile states, terrorism, climate change and the rise of new great powers. At the extreme, the integration of the global economy on which almost everybody now depends might be reversed.

## Addressing the Crisis

The decisions taken in the next year will shape the world for decades. So what has to be done? I suggest the following, focusing on the role of the International Monetary Fund [IMF].

First, we must realise that this is a crisis of the global economy that the US played a dominant role in creating. If that achievement, with all the promise it offers, is to survive, the crisis must be solved globally.

Second, the meeting of the G-20 heads of government in London [April 2009] is a recognition of this fact. Management of the world economy cannot be achieved by advanced economies alone. While not all the countries there present are systemically important, all systemically important countries will be there. The world looks for achievement at this summit. It must not be disappointed.

Third, the immediate priorities are to sustain demand, fix the global financial system and avoid a collapse into global protection. The longer-term aim must be to reconsider the regulation and structure of the financial system and reform the system of international economic and financial governance. Some progress has been made on these fronts. But it is not nearly enough.

Fourth, there is a very good chance that this crisis will lead to a much deeper decline in the world economy than is now expected and a slow and limping recovery. This risk must be eliminated, if at all possible.

Fifth, if the emerging economies are to trust themselves to the world economy, it is essential to offer generous help now. At the moment, they blame the West for what has happened. It has been helpful for the Fed and other central banks to advance loans to a few selected central banks. But much more is needed.

## The International Monetary Fund

Sixth, the current lending capacity of the IMF is about $250bn [billion], which is grossly inadequate. The US Treasury has proposed that this be raised to $750bn. That is the very least now needed. Remember that global foreign exchange reserves, predominantly held by emerging economies, rose from $1.5 trillion to $7 trillion between January 1999, after the Asian financial crisis, and their peak last year. This is an indication of the demand for reserves. It would be far more efficient, however, if reserves were pooled than if every country tried to insure itself, in this expensive way. That is what the IMF exists to do. It should be used for this purpose.

Seventh, in addition to increasing its resources, the governance of the IMF must be changed. Asian countries, in particular, still remember the humiliation treatment they received a decade ago at the hands of the IMF and the US treasury. They will want a much bigger say in the running of the Fund. An important step is a huge reduction in Europe's voting weights, which are now about a third of the total. Also important is an end to the traditional practice of having an American head the World Bank and a European head the IMF.

Eighth, serious thought must be given to making an annual allocation of SDRs (Special Drawing Rights)—the IMF's own reserve asset. This would satisfy the world's demand for reserves at no cost in resources. Traditionally, the US has regarded the SDR as a rival to the dollar as a reserve asset and treasured the ability to finance its external deficits through simple expansion of the supply of dollars. But the economic developments of the past decade should have shaken US complacency. The ability to run very large current account deficits has turned out to be a calamity, since, in my view, it offers a large part of the explanation for the current financial crisis in the US and so the world. Furthermore, the US needs to be able to export its way out of its current recession. Otherwise, it is likely to be stuck with a huge fiscal deficit for the indefinite future, to offset the higher domestic private saving and structural current account deficit. Increasing the purchasing power of emerging countries, through an annual allocation of about one trillion SDRs (a little less than 2 per cent of world GDP) would go a long way towards solving this problem. I fear that if this does not happen, a return to generalised protection would become likely, as a way for deficit countries, such as the US, to strengthen demand for domestic output and employment.

What I have outlined above is only a small part of the agenda. But it is a vital part. The more imaginative and energetic the US now is, the better able it will be to restore its reputation and influence across the globe. This is a time of decision. The US can either do everything in its power to restore and strengthen the global economic system it worked so hard to create. Choices must be made between outward-looking and inward-looking solutions. We tried the former in the 1930s. This time we should try the latter.

# The International Monetary Fund Must Play a Central Role in Ending the Financial Crisis

*George Soros*

*George Soros is founder and chairman of the Open Society Institute and the Soros Foundations Network, which work to build vibrant and tolerant democracies in which governments are accountable to their citizens.*

The current financial crisis is different from all the others we have experienced since the end of World War II. On previous occasions, whenever the financial system came to the brink of a breakdown, the authorities got their act together and prevented it from going over the brink. This time the system actually broke down when Lehman Brothers was allowed to fail on September 15, 2008. That event transformed what had been a mainly financial phenomenon into a calamity that affected the entire economy.

## The Center of the Crisis

Within days the financial system suffered what amounts to cardiac arrest and had to be put on artificial life support. That came as a shock to the business community and the general public. Everybody retrenched. International trade was particularly hard hit and is now down nearly $4 trillion from a year ago. The decline in employment has not yet hit the bottom, and the International Monetary Fund (IMF) estimates that globally more than 50 million people could lose their jobs by year end.

George Soros, "Testimony Before the Senate Foreign Relations Committee, Hearing on Foreign Policy and the Global Financial Crisis," Foreign.Senate.gov, March 25, 2009. Reproduced by permission of the author.

The countries on the periphery of the international financial system are even more severely affected than those at the center. The rich countries could effectively guarantee their financial institutions against default but the less developed countries, ranging from Eastern Europe to Africa, could not extend similarly convincing guarantees. As a result, capital is fleeing the periphery and it is difficult to roll over maturing loans. Exports suffer from the lack of trade finance. Deutsche Bank estimates that $1,440 billion of bank loans are coming due in 2009 alone.

The capital flight is abetted by national regulators intent on protecting their own financial systems by tacitly encouraging banks to repatriate funds. When history is written, it will be recorded that—in contrast to the Great Depression—protectionism first manifested itself in finance rather than trade. To stem the tide, the International Financial Institutions (IFIs) must be reinforced and reinvigorated. Unless effective measures are taken to protect the periphery countries against a storm that originated at the center, the international financial and trade system is liable to fall apart.

---

*China and the United States have a common interest in protecting the periphery countries from a storm that originated at the center.*

---

## The Responsibility of the United States

The primary responsibility lies with the United States, both because it is the originator of the crisis and because it enjoys veto rights in the IMF. It is not just a moral issue but a matter of self-interest. We have derived great benefits from being at the center of the global financial system and we ought to do whatever we can to preserve that position. If the multilateral system falls apart, every country will pursue its interests unilaterally. Then China will be much better situated than we are. While we are, regrettably, still lagging behind the curve in dealing with the crisis, China is ahead of the curve. Its banking system is in relatively good shape and it can activate its large stimulus program faster than we can ours. The leadership realizes that it must ensure economic growth in order to avoid social unrest and it is both willing and able to apply additional stimulus if the current program is not sufficient. To support its export industries it will extend credit to periphery countries just as it did to the United States. As things stand at present, China and the United States have a common interest in protecting the periphery countries from a storm that originated at the center. We must seize this opportunity even as we address our own recession.

While the primary responsibility is ours, we cannot act without the support of the European countries, which carry a disproportionate weight on the governing board of the IMF. Unfortunately, the IMF is ill-suited to the novel task with which it is now confronted. It is used to dealing with the failures of government policy, especially at the periphery; now it is confronted with the failure of the private sector at the center. To make matters worse, the IMF is deeply unpopular with public opinion both at the periphery and at the center—and that includes Congress. Moreover, there is a profound disagreement between the United States and Europe, particularly Germany, about the nature of the problem and the right remedies to apply.

## Germany's Opposition

The United States has recognized that the collapse of credit in the private sector can be reversed only by using the credit of the state to the full. Germany, traumatized by the memory of hyperinflation in the 1920s that led to the rise of Hitler in the 1930s, is reluctant to sow the seeds of future inflation by incurring too much debt. Both positions are firmly held and can be supported by valid arguments. In the case of Germany's opposition to the use of the German state's credit for the rest of Europe or the rest of the world, they are valid only from a narrow German point of view. Be that as it may, the controversy has dominated the preparations for the forthcoming G-20 meetings on April 2 [2009].

That meeting is a make or break event. Unless it comes up with practical measures to support the countries at the periphery of the global financial system, markets are going to suffer another sinking spell just as they did on February 10, 2009, when the authorities failed to produce practical measures to recapitalize the U.S. banking system. To put it in an oversimplified and exaggerated form, the United States wants to reinflate, Germany and Europe want to regulate. It should be possible, however, to find common ground in the need to protect the periphery countries from a calamity that is not of their own making. Actually, we need to both reinflate and regulate but reinflation is urgent and regulatory reforms will take time to implement. The urgent task has to be carried out mainly by the IMF, imperfect and beleaguered as it is, because it is the only institution available. The regulatory reforms will involve reforming the IMF and establishing other institutions.

*The fact is that the IMF simply does not have enough money to offer meaningful relief.*

## The Need for Funds

Periphery countries need to protect their financial systems including trade finance and to enable them to engage in countercyclical fiscal policies. The former requires large contingency funds available at short notice for relatively short periods of time. The latter requires long-term financing.

When the adverse side effects of the Lehman bankruptcy on the periphery countries became evident, the IMF introduced a new short-term liquidity (STL) facility that allows countries that are otherwise in sound financial condition to borrow five times their quota for three months without any conditionality. But the size of the STL is too small to be of much use, especially while a potential stigma associated with the use of IMF funds lingers. That is now being remedied, but even if it worked, any help for the top-tier countries would merely aggravate the situation of the lower-tier countries. International assistance to enable periphery countries to engage in countercyclical policies has not even been considered.

The fact is that the IMF simply does not have enough money to offer meaningful relief. It has about $200 billion in uncommitted funds at its disposal, and the potential needs are much greater. As things stand now, the G-20 meeting can be expected to produce some concrete results: The resources of the IMF are likely to be effectively doubled, mainly by using the mechanism of the New Arrangements to Borrow (NAB), which can be activated without resolving the vexing question of reapportioning voting rights in the IFIs. NAB will require congressional approval.

## Special Drawing Rights

The capital increase will be sufficient to enable the IMF to come to the aid of specific countries in difficulties, but it will not provide a systemic solution for the developing world. Periphery countries are reluctant to apply to the IMF for support as seen from the fact that the recently introduced short-term liquidity facility that allows qualified countries to borrow *without* any conditionality has had no takers. A more radical solution is needed. Such a solution is readily available in the form of Special Drawing Rights (SDRs). The mechanism exists and has already been used on a small scale. There is a pending issue of SDR 21.4 billion ($32.2 billion), which only requires approval by the United States to become effective.

SDRs are highly complicated and difficult to understand but they boil down to the international creation of money. Countries that are in a position to create their own money do not need them but the periphery countries do. The rich countries should therefore lend their allocations to the countries in need. This would not create a budget deficit for them. The recipient countries would have to pay the IMF interest at a very low rate: the composite average treasury bill rate of all convertible currencies. They would have free use of their own allocations, but the IFIs would supervise how the borrowed allocations are used. (The World Bank, which has devoted a lot of resources to developing poverty alleviation programs, would be better suited for this task than the IMF). This should ensure that the borrowed funds are well spent. It is difficult to think of a scheme where the cost/benefit ratio is so favorable.

In addition to a onetime increase in the IMF's resources there ought to be substantial annual SDR issues, say $250 billion, as long as the global recession lasts. To make the scheme countercyclical, the SDR issues could be callable in tranches [installments] when the global economy overheats. It is too late to agree on issuing SDRs at the April 2 G-20 meeting, but if it were raised by President Obama and endorsed by others, it would be sufficient to give heart to the markets and turn the April 2 meeting into a resounding success. [The G-20 authorized $250 billion in new SDRs at that meeting.]

---

*The IMF is far from perfect, but it is more needed than ever.*

---

The SDR proposal, arcane as it is, makes eminent sense. The United States and Europe are actively engaged in creating money to replace credit. SDRs would provide money to less-developed countries that cannot create their own—at no cost to those who make their allocations available.

## The Need for the IMF

One of the obstacles standing in the way is the well-known negative attitude of Congress toward anything connected with the IMF. The SDR issue does not require legislation. Nevertheless, it would be very helpful if Congress expressed a willingness to authorize the NAB, which does require congressional approval, and supported the SDR issue in principle.

As we have seen, the IMF is far from perfect, but it is more needed than ever. It has a new mission in life: to assist the less-developed countries to protect their banking systems and enable them to engage in countercyclical fiscal polices. How well it fulfills that mission will have a major impact both on the survival of the international financial and trading system and on our leadership position within that system.

# The International Monetary Fund Cannot End the Financial Crisis

*Desmond Lachman*

*Desmond Lachman is a resident fellow at the American Enterprise Institute for Public Policy Research and previously served as deputy director of the International Monetary Fund's Policy Development and Review Department.*

L ast week's G-20 heads of state meeting [April 2, 2009] took place against the backdrop of the worst global economic crisis in the postwar period. Yet judging by that meeting's meager results—largely limited to an increase in the size of the International Monetary Fund—one could be excused for thinking that the G-20 must believe that whatever might presently be ailing the global economy can be readily fixed with an IMF [International Monetary Fund] Band-Aid. One has to hope that global policy makers get much more serious about the present economic crisis or the world economy will find itself caught in a deflationary trap.

Since the G-20 meeting in Washington last November, the world economy has sunk much deeper into a synchronized recession on a scale not experienced in the postwar period. GDP [gross domestic product] is now contracting at more than a 6 percent annualized rate in the United States and Europe, while it is declining at annualized double-digit rates in Japan. The Organisation for Economic Co-operation and Development (OECD) is now forecasting that the industrialized countries will contract by more than 4 percent in 2009, which would mark their worst economic performance in the last 60 years. Compounding matters has been a collapse in international trade that raises the real specter of a return to the destructive protectionist policies of the 1930s.

## The Real Problems

Most economists would agree that the two primary factors driving the global economic recession have been a severe asset price bust and a "once in a lifetime" credit-market crunch in the major industrialized countries. As an indication of the severity of the decline in global equity and housing prices, the OECD now estimates that approximately US$50 trillion in global household wealth, or the equivalent of around 100 percent of world GDP, has been wiped out over the past year. As an indication of the severity of the banking crisis, the IMF estimates that the total losses to the global banking system from bad lending practices will amount to US$2.3 trillion, or more than double the losses that the banks have recognized to date.

The most striking aspect of the recently concluded G-20 meeting was its failure to make any progress in dealing with the real problems afflicting the global economy. For, despite all the spin that policy makers are putting on the meeting, no agreement was reached on the additional fiscal policy stimulus so sorely needed to offset the ravages of falling asset prices on global household expenditures. And the meeting also failed to come up with any new initiatives that might adequately recapitalize the global financial system, another necessary condition for starting a sustainable global economic recovery.

## The International Monetary Fund

While the G-20 meeting was unable to reach agreement on the real issues presently afflicting the global economy, it did make substantial progress in increasing the size of the IMF. Indeed, the G-20 credibly pledged to treble the size of the IMF from US$250 billion to US$750 billion and to effect a US$250 billion additional allocation of Special Drawing

Rights, the IMF's unit of account. The question remains, however, whether this agreement was more than a fig leaf to hide the lack of progress on the more substantive challenges facing the global economy, and whether by itself it can do very much to staunch the bleeding.

---

*Increasing the IMF's resources does virtually nothing to ameliorate the unprecedented slump presently afflicting the world's major industrialized countries.*

---

To be sure, the prospective enlargement of the IMF's lending capability should be helpful in cushioning the blow of the global economic crisis on the emerging market economies in general and on those in Eastern Europe in particular. With substantially increased loanable resources, the IMF can be more effective in shoring up the external finances of these countries as they grapple with shrinking export markets and with a sudden drying up in capital inflows from abroad.

## The Industrialized Countries

The key point, however, is that increasing the IMF's resources does virtually nothing to ameliorate the unprecedented slump presently afflicting the world's major industrialized countries. And until one gets a meaningful recovery in those countries, the emerging market economies will continue to be under severe pressure. They will remain so as they find their export markets continuing to shrink, their commodity prices continuing to decline, and their foreign bankers reluctant to roll over their loans.

If ever there was a time that global economic policy coordination was needed to prevent the world sliding deeper into recession it has to be now. However, judging by the meager results of yet another G-20 meeting one has to wonder whether a smaller forum comprised of the world's four major economies—the United States, Japan, China, and Germany—

might not be better suited to get meaningful policy coordination among the countries that really count for the global economy. One also has to wonder whether the global economy has the luxury of waiting another six months before the G-20 has another go at getting its act together.

**CONTROVERSIES**

# CHAPTER 3

# Is Globalization of the World Economy Good for the World?

# Overview: Globalization of the World Economy

## Joseph Campbell

*Joseph Campbell is a contributing editor of* Catholic Insight.

Globalization is one of the buzz words of contemporary economics. Defined as the creation of a single world market for goods and services, globalization is transforming the planet's economy by dramatically stimulating international trade and investment. Undergirding this process is the electronics revolution, by means of which billions of dollars can move into and out of economies at the stroke of a key.

Is it good? Archbishop Francois Nguyen Van Thuan, president of the Pontifical Council for Justice and Peace, points out that the results of globalization have been both positive and negative. "The social doctrine of the Church," he says, "suggests that we understand this phenomenon as a sign of the times. . . ." The dimensions are "broad and profound, typical of the history of this period of humanity.

"The Church does not condemn the liberalization of the market, but it appeals for respect for the primacy of the human person, to whom all economic systems must be subject."

## Pope John Paul II's View on Globalization

Pope John Paul II sees globalization as both economic and political. For all its risks, he says, it offers exceptional and promising opportunities. These should enable humanity to become "a single family, built on the values of justice, equity and solidarity." This, however, requires a complete change of

Joseph Campbell, "Globalization and Social Justice," *Catholic Insight*, May 1, 2001, p. 14.

perspective. "It is no longer the well-being of any one political, racial or cultural community that must prevail, but rather the good of humanity as a whole." What this means is that "the pursuit of the common good of a single political community cannot be in conflict with the common good of humanity." The principle of solidarity, which promotes the common good, at the same time advances the individual good, particularly that of the weakest and poorest. The pope says solidarity must be made an integral part of the network of economic, political and social interdependence that globalization tends to consolidate. A commitment to solidarity makes the poor the agents of their own development. It "enables the greatest number of people, in their specific economic and political circumstances, to exercise the creativity which is characteristic of the human person. . . ." The pope recognizes that the wealth of nations depends on this creativity. His Holiness cites the dire poverty of countless millions of men and women as the issue which most challenges our human and Christian consciences. He states that because humanity, called to form a single family, is tragically split in two by poverty, we urgently need to reconsider the models which inspire policies of development.

We also need to foster "a consciousness of universal moral values" to face challenges that are assuming an increasingly global dimension. These include:

- the promotion of peace and human rights;

- the settling of armed conflicts within states and across borders;

- the protection of ethnic minorities and immigrants;

- the safeguarding of the environment;

- the battles against disease, drug and arms trafficking;

- and political and economic corruption.

These issues, which concern the entire human community, must be faced and resolved through common efforts. No nation is in a position to face them alone.

---

*Due to globalization, proponents say, most major developed nations and many emerging markets have experienced prolonged economic growth.*

---

We must find a way to discuss humanity's problems in "a comprehensible and common language." The basis of such a dialogue, the pope says, is natural law, "the universal moral law written upon the human heart." He states that by following this "grammar" of the spirit, "the human community can confront the problems of coexistence and move forward to the future with respect for God's plan."

A fair interpretation of the foregoing is that the Church is offering its social teaching as a basis for the global economy and for international political institutions up to and including a world government.

## The Positives and Negatives of Globalization

Positives and negatives of globalization, actual and anticipated, are being widely discussed. Economically, proponents credit the more open and integrated markets with dramatic increases in world trade, vast new business opportunities, record levels of foreign business investment, and more jobs. Due to globalization, proponents say, most major developed nations and many emerging markets have experienced prolonged economic growth. Moreover, inflation is said to be much lower than it would otherwise have been. This is attributed in part to the entry of new competitors into the more open markets, which has helped to keep prices down.

Opponents of economic globalization say that it is enabling a relatively few transnational corporations to shape national and international law to suit their interests. Under international trade agreements, tribunals set up to resolve disputes supersede the legal systems of nation states and supplant their judicial processes. This, the opponents state, undermines the democratic basis of our legal systems, threatens public social programs, and limits the ability of governments, among other things, to protect the environment and safeguard human rights.

Some opponents have blamed whimsical or irrational global speculation for financial crises in Asia, Russia and Latin America. Others criticize transnational monopolies for shifting production to areas where labour is cheapest, taxes are lowest and controls are weakest.

Politically, proponents of globalization are heartened by international agencies and initiatives that seek to limit war and promote universal respect for human rights. The establishment of an international criminal court to try crimes against humanity regardless of where they are committed is considered a major step forward.

Critics are concerned lest proponents of militant secularism and moral individualism gain control of international agencies. As national sovereignty defers to world government, these agencies could overrule individual and communal efforts to promote traditional religion and morality. This is already beginning, in fact, as national governments face pressure from United Nations agencies to impose contraception, abortion, homosexual privileges, and questionable affirmative action.

## Economic Globalization

If economic globalization is to contribute to the civilization of love which the Church fosters, it must empower the poor to create wealth, as the pope has indicated. No matter how substantial, grants of money, loans, and even windfall profits cannot guarantee success in this endeavour.

Consider the experience of the Arab nations. During the sixteen years following the OPEC [Organization of the Petroleum Exporting Countries] supply restrictions of 1973, these countries earned an estimated two trillion dollars by exporting oil. Writing in 1990, Sever Plotzker . . . [chief economic editor of *Yedioth Ahronoth*] said this could have turned the region into an economic power and ensured its future.

---

*Money, even in large amounts, does not produce economic activism.*

---

The Arabs, however, invested very little of it in "industrial, educational, and social infrastructure that would prepare . . . for the post-windfall era to come." As a result, "The economic situation, except for Saudi Arabia and the Gulf, is . . . very bad. Education per capita is on the decline. . . . There is no industry, let alone the high-tech or export kind. The dynamic Asian states have overtaken the Arab world even though they do not produce oil (except for Indonesia). There are few productive jobs."

The intriguing question is "Where did all the money go?" Plotzker estimates that the Arabs spent at least half of it on wars and armies and much of the rest on risky investments and "showy projects devoid of economic sense or logic."

In the West, the shock of higher oil prices contributed to inflation, unemployment, and a prolonged economic slump. World Bank economist Alan Gelb concluded that since most of the oil-exporting nations were worse off than before the boom, the era of windfall profits constituted a massive net loss for the whole world.

Money, even in large amounts, does not produce economic activism. Economic activism produces money. The Arab experience and the history of official foreign aid confirm this. In the absence of wealth-creating strategies, huge transfers of money are ineffective.

The strategies of wealth creation are no secret. You can see them at work in the West and in Japan and some of the other Asian states. Each implements them in its own way and in accordance with its traditions and culture. Other nations could do the same. What they basically require is a legal system and institutions that reward rather than discourage economic initiative among the masses.

---

*When political and economic arrangements are conducive to development, people can be expected to respond accordingly.*

---

## Specific Strategies

Specific strategies include incentives for widespread ownership of enterprises, easy and inexpensive incorporation of small businesses, relief from excessive taxation and oppressive regulation of agriculture and commerce, ready access to credit to finance productive activities, protection of patents and copyrights to encourage innovation, investment in universal education and training at all levels, privatization of state enterprises where these command a disproportionate share of the economy, and financial policies that maintain the soundness of currencies and discourage capital flight.

Such strategies and institutional arrangements set the stage for development. Equally important are the individual and social attributes—self-reliance, discipline, perseverance, cooperativeness, belief in the future—required to focus initiative and effort on economic advancement. Mores, values, attitudes, social institutions, and political structures, as well as individual aptitudes, are crucial.

When political and economic arrangements are conducive to development, people can be expected to respond accordingly. They did it in the West and they are doing it in the emerging economies of the East. Because of cultural and other differences, some societies will move faster and do better than others. But all that want to develop can learn how. The creativity that fuels economic advancement is a fundamental and universal human good.

## International Lending and Borrowing

Massive third world debt has been identified as a barrier to economic development and an oppressive burden on the poor. In 1994, the pope proposed that we consider reducing, if not cancelling, international debts that threaten the future of many countries. Debt relief, he said, would be an appropriate initiative for the Jubilee of the Year 2000. Social activists, both religious and secular, are campaigning to have these debts forgiven, and world leaders are responding. Last September [2000], the pope stressed that the benefits of debt relief must reach the poorest. This should be done "through a sustained and comprehensive framework of investment in the capacities of human persons, especially through education and health care."

He described debt relief as a precondition for the poorest countries to make progress in their fight against poverty. But he said that it must be accompanied by "the introduction of sound economic policies and good governance."

The last point is crucial, because unsound financial policies and government corruption have too often characterized international lending and borrowing. Over the last half century, both public and private agencies have loaned hundreds of billions of dollars internationally, often with a shocking lack of due diligence. Much of the money went directly into the pockets of corrupt officials, helped third world elites oppress the already downtrodden, or financed grandiose vanity projects that held little prospect of providing a return on investment. First world lenders can afford to be reckless in their financial dealings when they are confident that governments—that is to say taxpayers—will bail them out.

And we have bailed them out. Not only do we stand behind the World Bank and the International Monetary Fund, but we have already come to the rescue of the Chase Manhattans and Citicorps for much of the reckless private-sector lending that precipitated past third world debt crises.

Unless we remove the inducements to irrational lending, debt cancellation will be a mixed blessing. It will relieve the third world poor of repaying loans that failed to help and often harmed them; but it will also reward first world lenders for their lack of due diligence and encourage them to float similar loans, whose risks, they know, will be underwritten by Western taxpayers.

So yes, for moral and economic reasons we should forgive much of the third world debt. For similar reasons, we should make lenders, not taxpayers, assume the risks of future loans. If they are made fully accountable, as private lending agencies usually are for domestic loans, international lenders will be disinclined to underwrite economically unsound activities and projects.

If we are moving toward one world, politically as well as economically, we must strive mightily to avoid the errors of the past. It would be tragic, indeed, if we created a global welfare state with massive bureaucracies and publicly funded interest groups dedicated to coercive social engineering in the service of secularism, amorality or worse. To avoid that, and promote a civilization of reason, morality and love, we must embrace natural law, as the pope indicated, and safeguard genuine religious freedom. This, I submit, should be a prerequisite for the establishment of any world government. In particular, we must entrench in a global constitution the principle of subsidiarity. This principle respects the autonomy of communities in areas which are properly theirs, and protects them from the intrusions of distant and often unaccountable agencies.

# Globalization Raises Everyone's Standard of Living

*Gennady Stolyarov II*

*Gennady Stolyarov II is an essayist and editor in chief of the* Rational Argumentator, *an Internet journal that champions the principles of reason, rights, and progress.*

Much of the prosperity of today's world arises from the division of labor. Globalization, by extending the market's scope to the entire world, enables the division of labor to become as developed as the current world population allows. However, to be truly in the interests of consumers and a boon to economic prosperity, globalization needs to occur spontaneously through the workings of the unhampered free market. Government attempts to meddle with this process— even with the sincere intent to facilitate or accelerate it—will only undermine its efficacy at benefiting us all.

## The Division of Labor

In his 1776 classic, *The Wealth of Nations*, Adam Smith explained that "the division of labor is limited by the extent of the market." This is not hard to understand on an individual and local scale. Imagine you are somewhat skilled at making tables. If you live alone in a cabin in the woods and can only personally use the tables you make, you might create four or five of them—but there your need for them would stop. You would have little further reason to continually develop your table-making skills. You would not be able to turn table-making into your full time occupation. After all, you also need food, shelter, non-table furniture, and myriad other goods to have even a meager standard of living. You would have to cre-

Gennady Stolyarov II, "Globalization: Extending the Market and Human Well-Being," *Freeman: Ideas on Liberty*, vol. 59, April 2009, pp. 26–30. Copyright © 2009 Foundation for Economic Education. Reproduced by permission. www.thefreemanonline.org.

ate all these goods yourself, with no time to develop anything beyond a rudimentary table-making ability.

If you have a few friends who also use tables, you can devote more of your time to making them and improving your craftsmanship, while exchanging the tables for other goods your friends specialize in producing. If you live in a village, your ability to obtain most of the goods you desire solely by producing tables increases along with your likelihood of finding enough people who demand tables to keep you busy during all of your working hours. As you sharpen your skills, you might even begin to incorporate artistic flourishes into your tables and learn how to make tables suited to specific purposes. Perhaps you might become a master craftsman of coffee tables or desks. In a large city, the demand for either of these types of tables alone might keep you employed.

---

*Improved transportation and communication technology enable previously formidable barriers of distance and geography to be overcome.*

---

But imagine that your passion in life is to carve elaborate geometric designs into your tables and turn them into unique works of art. This kind of table-making takes many days of hard work, and only a few people in the world would appreciate the merits of your table art. You might be able to command a high price for each of your special tables—say, $10,000—if you could find a buyer. But let us say that only 60 people out of the world population of six billion would be willing buyers of one of your tables each year. In your large city, there are six million people, so your probability of finding even one buyer in your city would be a mere 0.06—giving you an expected annual income of $600 if you specialized in making your unique tables. But if you were able to access customers from all over the *world* easily, then you might fulfill all the existing demand for your work and thereby receive an annual income of $600,000. You can live lavishly by only serving the needs of 60 people—*if* your market extends to the entire world. If you could only sell in your city, you would likely never have made many of your special tables, leaving so much potential value uncreated.

## Three Factors

Globalization is the process of the ever-increasing extension of markets, past national and even regional boundaries. Three principal factors drive globalization. First, improved transportation and communication technology enable previously formidable barriers of distance and geography to be overcome. Adam Smith remarked on the extent to which water transport facilitated the division of labor and consumers' ability to get more and better goods faster: "A broad-wheeled wagon, attended by two men, and drawn by eight horses, in about six weeks' time carries and brings back between London and Edinburgh near four ton weight of goods. In about the same time a ship navigated by six or eight men, and sailing between the ports of London and Leith, frequently carries and brings back two hundred ton weight of goods." In our age, air freight and the Internet can be added to the list of technologies facilitating the extent of the market.

*People in globalizing markets begin to extend increasing respect, understanding, and willingness to cooperate to those who are unlike them.*

The second factor facilitating globalization is the removal of government restrictions on trade. Tariffs, quotas, subsidies to domestic producers, and other trade barriers make it difficult for businesses located outside a country to compete with domestic producers based solely on the consumer-evaluated merits of their products. Such interventionist measures tax domestic consumers and foreign businesses and artificially inflate the incomes of some—though by far not all—domestic businesses. The favored businesses have reduced incentives to cut costs and increase product quality, since the government shields them from the most intense competition. In the long run, this leads to poor products, widespread waste, organizational inefficiency, and consumer dissatisfaction. When government trade barriers are removed and no regulations are put in their place this burden is lifted from millions of consumers and producers, who are now able to extend the market to the degree desired by consumers. Since reaching a high point with the Smoot-Hawley Tariff Act of 1930, tariffs levied by the United States against imported goods have generally declined up to the present day. Tariffs and other protectionist policies in many other countries have been likewise reduced, especially from the 1980s onward.

The third factor responsible for globalization is increased tolerance by people throughout the world for others of different national, ethnic, and cultural backgrounds. As trade among people begins to take place, it becomes easier for people to see one another in terms of the goods and services they offer, rather than in terms of negative stereotypes, hatreds, and fear of "the other." In a virtuous cycle, people in globalizing markets begin to extend increasing respect, understanding, and willingness to cooperate to those who are unlike them. A more cosmopolitan, individualistic outlook emerges: Each producer and consumer is judged on the basis of personal actions and merits, not circumstantial group identity. This in turn makes it much easier for people to engage in trade with still more others, unhindered by unwarranted negative preconceptions. The prevalence in the United States of Mexican food, Japanese automobiles and electronics, Chinese manufactured goods, South American fruits, and hundreds of thousands of other goods imported from virtually all parts of the world illustrates the seamless merger between economic and cultural exchange—a ubiquitous characteristic of globalization. Richard Cobden, perhaps the most outspoken free trade advocate of the nineteenth century, saw this growth of tolerance as a desirable aim and outcome of the extension of trade: "The people of [France and England] must be brought into mutual dependence by the supply of each others' wants. There is no other way of counteracting the antagonism of language and race . . . and no other plan is worth a farthing."

## More Variety

The benefits of globalization are manifold. Economists recognize that globalization lowers prices for a wide array of consumer goods, thereby making consumers better off in real terms. But increased product variety is another outcome, well documented by Christian Broda and David Weinstein in their 2006 *Quarterly Journal of Economics* paper, "Globalization and the Gains from Variety." Broda and Weinstein note that "in 1972 the US imported 74,667 varieties (i.e., 7,731 goods from an average of 9.7 countries) and in 2001 there were 259,215 varieties (16,390 goods from an average of 15.8 countries)." Some of these goods were already common in their regions of origin but have now been able to spread elsewhere and find willing consumers. The spread of other products was only made possible by the ability of their providers to find enough customers by extending their market to the entire world. In his essay "Spicing the Gains from Globalization with Product Variety," Neel Chamilall emphasizes "that consumers value this greater product variety for its own sake, on top of the lower prices that globalization also generates." A wider range of possible satisfactions is valued since the more kinds of products exist, the likelier a particular product is to fulfill the specific tastes of an individual consumer at any given moment.

But globalization's extension of the market facilitates more than the production of greater numbers and varieties of material goods. The *intellectual* division of labor—as well as the opportunities for intellectual cooperation extending throughout the world—are also greatly magnified by globalization. In "Globalization: The Long-Run Big Picture," George Reisman explains that globalization brings about a "substantial increase in the number of highly intelligent, highly motivated individuals working in all of the branches of science, technology, and business. This will greatly accelerate the rate of scientific and technological progress and business innovation." Reisman observes that "one of the greatest of all gains that results from the division of labor is the ability of geniuses to devote their full time to activities representing the discovery and application of new knowledge." The broader the division of labor, the greater the likelihood that a creative genius in business, science, medicine, engineering, or another vital field will not personally need to manufacture most of the goods he desires. Moreover, the likelihood that he will find a market receptive to his own endeavors increases to the maximum extent if he can interact with anyone in the world.

---

*As everyone is enabled to participate in a truly global division of labor, its benefits will spread throughout the world.*

---

## Benefits for All

When creative geniuses—or creative people in general—communicate with one another, exchange ideas, and build on one another's work, additional economies of scale emerge. Many creators relying on each other's utmost strengths can produce more discoveries, inventions, structures, and organizational innovations than the sum total produced by each creator working in complete isolation—just as the division of labor in the pin factories Adam Smith observed could raise the number of pins produced per worker by orders of magnitude. When national, geographic, and cultural boundaries no longer pose barriers to creators exchanging ideas and undertaking joint ventures, some of the greatest possible benefits to all humanity can be realized.

If globalization proceeds unhampered, it will achieve, in Reisman's words, "the elevation of the productivity of labor and of living standards all across the globe to the level of the most advanced countries, and at the same time the radical improvement in productivity and living standards in what are today the most advanced countries." As everyone is enabled to participate in a truly global division of labor, its benefits will spread throughout the world—eradicating true poverty and much other human suffering in all areas where governments do not forcibly restrain their people from peaceful economic and cultural exchange.

---

*International institutions devised by Western governments allegedly to promote deregulation and globalization have often achieved the opposite purpose.*

---

## No Government Intervention

But aside from staying out of globalization's way, governments cannot act efficaciously to promote or accelerate it. As George Washington is reputed to have said, "Government is not reason. It is not eloquence. Government is force; like fire it is a dangerous servant—and a fearful master." Government's entire modus operandi is force or the threat thereof. If the government promotes *anything* in an affirmative fashion, it can only do so through the use of force. Calling a particular exertion of government force a "free trade agreement" or a "free trade organization" does not alter its nature, and the facts attest to this. In "Can Trade Ever Harm a Country?" Robert P. Murphy comments on the NAFTA "free trade agreement": "The NAFTA [North American Free Trade Agreement] is over 1,000 pages, detailing all sorts of environmental and labor regulations and establishing supranational boards to rule on disputes. If NAFTA really did nothing but establish free trade, it would be the size of a postcard, and there would currently be no tariffs between Mexico and the U.S." It is true that NAFTA lowers some tariffs and lifts other trade restrictions, but the government's *affirmative* exertions in this agreement amount to regulating and intervening *more* in certain aspects of commerce by controlling thousands of tiny elements of production, employment, and property ownership that would otherwise have been left to individual choice. There is no clear way of determining that the "free trade agreement" resulted in more freedom than would have existed otherwise.

International institutions devised by Western governments allegedly to promote deregulation and globalization have often achieved the opposite purpose. Much of the apparatus of the World Trade Organization (WTO) engages in the imposition of retaliatory tariffs on the products of countries whose governments are deemed uncooperative. From a free market standpoint, this is a travesty. Because the *government* of a particular country has infringed on economic freedoms, must the *private individuals and businesses* of that country suffer further infringements of their freedoms as a result? Moreover, having tariffs imposed through the WTO merely legitimizes them and falsely assures many who would otherwise have opposed them that trade barriers are necessary somehow to bring about free trade.

## Unilateral Action That Works

The only legitimate government policy regarding globalization is to *let the process develop* spontaneously through the interactions of billions of private individuals and to lift all trade restrictions *unilaterally*. Even if other governments have tremendous trade restrictions against American producers, and even if they completely prohibit imports into their countries, the U.S. government should permit all foreign goods to enter the country without at all taxing them, restricting their quantity, or regulating their quality.

The reasons for unilateral renunciation of all trade restrictions become clear once one considers that American consumers are subject to two distinct sources of harm. The first source is the trade barriers set up by other governments. But trade restrictions established by the *United States* government perpetrate even greater damage to American consumers, resulting directly in higher prices and lower quality. The presumption behind multilateral "free trade agreements" has been that *only* foreign-imposed trade barriers hurt domestic consumers, while domestically imposed trade barriers are simply defensive or retaliatory measures. But if *both* foreign and domestic trade barriers hurt domestic consumers, then it is always preferable to have just one of these sources of harm—the foreign trade barriers—instead of both.

---

*The way to truly accelerate globalization is ... to boldly proceed alone in knocking down one domestic trade barrier after another.*

---

The benefits of unilateral renunciation of trade restrictions do not stop at freeing consumers from domestically imposed tariffs, quotas, regulations, and subsidies. Such a course of government *inaction* sends an unambiguous message to foreign governments and businesses that we are willing to benefit from anything they have to offer us, while respecting them enough to let them operate as they see fit. This gesture of goodwill is likely to be reciprocated, just as Cobden's success in getting Britain to abolish the Corn Laws unilaterally in 1848 led multiple European countries to eliminate many of their own trade barriers.

The way to truly accelerate globalization is not to wait for all nations to agree warily to the conditional removal of restraints on their own people, but rather to boldly proceed alone in knocking down one domestic trade barrier after another. With the passage of time, it will become evident that not having retaliatory trade restrictions against the producers of other countries does *not* in fact harm American consumers or producers. Other governments, seeing the mercantilist fears falsified empirically, will become increasingly inclined to join in the rising prosperity by opening their markets to globalization. As globalization fosters a truly international division of labor, billions of people will come to benefit from unprecedented product variety, technological growth, and cultural exchange.

# Globalization Is Good for the Poor of the World

*Rich Lowry*

*Rich Lowry is editor of the* National Review *and is a syndicated columnist.*

Global capitalism has long lacked for a ringing slogan like "workers of the world unite." It's never too late to find one, and a good candidate—with apologies to the international charity of the same name—might be "save the children."

## Economic Growth and Child Mortality

The United Nations Children's Fund [UNICEF] just announced that deaths of young children worldwide hit an all-time low, falling beneath ten million annually. Better practices to protect against disease and to enhance nutrition—more vaccinations and mosquito nets, more breast-feeding and vitamin A drops—played a role, but the most important factor in this global good-news story is economic growth.

It is no coincidence that as UNICEF was reporting the drop in child mortality, the World Bank was reporting global poverty rates had fallen as part of an extraordinary worldwide economic boom. Treasury Secretary Henry Paulson calls it "far and away the strongest global economy I've seen in my business lifetime." The global economy is growing at a 5-percent

Rich Lowry, "Do It for the Children," *National Review Online*, September 21, 2007. Copyright © 2007 by National Review, Inc., 215 Lexington Avenue, New York, NY 10016. Reproduced by permission.

clip, higher than the 3 percent of the period from 1960 to 1980 and the 4.7 percent from 1960 to 1980. As *U.S. News & World Report* points out, "Gross global product is three times as big as it was in 1970"; so the global economy is not only growing faster, but there's more to grow.

In a worldwide instance of trickle-down economics, the growth is diminishing the ranks of the poor. According to the World Bank, developing countries have averaged 3.9 percent growth since 2000, contributing "to rapidly falling poverty rates in all developing regions over the past few years." In 1990, 1.25 billion people lived on less than $1 a day. In 2004, less than a billion did, even though world population increased 20 percent in the interim.

## Wealth and Health

When a developing country gets richer, it means that people living there are less likely to be malnourished and—as infrastructure improves—more likely to have access to clean water and to sanitation. This is a boon to health.

A recent article in the journal *Lancet* concluded that "undernutrition is the underlying cause of a substantial proportion of all child deaths." Malnutrition weakens a child's immune system and makes him more susceptible to diarrhea, malaria, pneumonia and other diseases. Lack of potable water and sanitation—roughly one billion people lack clean water, and two billion lack sanitation—also increases the risk of illness, obviously. Millions die every year from diseases associated with contaminated water and poor sanitation.

China and India have led the way in growth, with the fastest- and second-fastest-growing major economies in the world. Thus, what have been sinks of human misery on a vast scale for centuries are becoming more livable. China accounted for almost all the recent drop in people living on less than $1 a day, experiencing a decline of 300 million since 1990. India has seen its mortality rate for children under the age of 5 decline from 123 per 1,000 in 1990 to 74 in 2005.

## Globalization Saves Lives

Such growth in developing countries is the result of, according to the World Bank, "further integration into world markets, better functioning internal markets and rising demand for many commodities." In short: globalization and capitalism. When a goateed anarcho-syndicalist commits an act of vandalism at an anti-globalization protest, he might think that he's striking a blow against The Man, but he's really rallying against the chance some desperately poor little boy or girl has to live a healthier life.

Because we in the West have reached the sunny uplands of sustained economic development, we can worry about the deleterious second-order effects—pollution, etc.—of growth. In too many places around the world, however, economic growth is still a matter of life and death. Governments, philanthropists, and activists have been pouring massive resources into fighting AIDS and other diseases in the third world recently. This is all very commendable, but we can't ignore the main event.

By all means, let's save the world—help it grow.

# A Small Minority of People in the World Benefit from Globalization

*Rainer Falk*

*Rainer Falk is the publisher of the Web site* World Economy & Development in Brief, *an information service on globalization, North-South relations, and international ecology.*

So far, only a small minority of top earners has benefited from global integration. Even conservative economists have begun to worry about social inclusion and effective redistribution. As many argue, it is better to prevent protectionist tendencies, which would cut the overall benefits of globalisation, and to share the cake more fairly.

## Worries About Globalisation

Immanuel Wallerstein and Stephen Roach are miles apart ideologically. But they pretty much agree on one thing: After three decades of globalisation euphoria, the pendulum has begun to swing back. "The political balance is swinging back," writes world-system's analyst Immanuel Wallerstein. "Neoliberal globalisation will be discussed about ten years from now as a cyclical swing in the history of the capitalist world economy. The real question is not whether this phase is over but whether the swing will be able, as in the past, to restore a state of relative equilibrium in the world system." Where Wallerstein sees the end of neoliberal globalisation, the chairman of Morgan Stanley, Asia, Stephen Roach, sees an about-turn: "What I suspect is that a partial backtracking is probably now at hand, as the collective interests of globalisation succumb to the self-interests of 'localisation'. An era of localisa-

Rainer Falk, "Spreading the Benefits of Globalisation: In Preventing the Big Backlash," *World Economy & Development in Brief*, March-April 2008. Reproduced by permission.

tion will undoubtedly have some very different characteristics from trends of the recent past. The most obvious: Wages could go up and corporate profits could come under pressure."

It remains to be seen whether or not "localisation" is the appropriate term to describe current trends. But it is indisputable that more and more people are questioning that globalisation has delivered on its promises and benefits. In a recent survey, 57% of the people polled in the G-7 nations said that globalisation has moved too fast over the past few years. Of those polled in 27 other countries, 64% thought that the advantages and burdens of globalisation were shared unfairly. Only in a few countries (10 out of 34) did the majority of people consider globalisation a positive factor for local economic development.

These countries included, significantly, the catch-up economies of China and Russia, the beneficiaries of soaring oil prices such as the United Arab Emirates or special cases in the OECD [Organisation of Economic Co-operation and Development] like Canada and Australia.

## Globalisation and Inequality

Poll results are always easy to challenge. But in this case, they match the latest trends of debate among economists and international development agencies. This debate revolves around the extent to which inequality in and between nations is linked to globalisation and international economic integration. The concern about increasing inequality triggering backlashes against global integration has spread to orthodox economists. Earlier, they only used to discuss the benefits of globalisation.

Economists Kenneth F. Scheve and Matthew J. Slaughter are two examples. The latter served on the Council of Economic Advisers of US President George Bush from 2005 to 2007. In an essay in *Foreign Affairs* last year [2007], both authors called for a "New Deal" for globalisation, based on new, top-down redistribution policies, in order to allow the vast majority a share in the benefits of globalisation. It is noteworthy that this debate is not only being conducted with a view to the traditional North-South divide, but rather emphasises domestic trends in rich nations.

Development policy makers noticed the problems first. Three years ago [2005], three reports by multilateral institutions simultaneously focused on the growing social inequality both within and among the nations of the world. The title of the World Development Report of 2006 was "Equity and Development". In it, the World Bank acknowledged that redistribution of income, as well as growth, is needed to reduce global poverty. Meanwhile, the UN's Report on the World Social Situation and the UNDP's [United Nations Development Programme's] Human Development Report highlighted the importance of distribution issues for achieving the Millennium Development Goals (MDGs).

---

*Both global inequality and global poverty are vastly greater than previously assumed.*

---

## Inequality and Poverty

The International Monetary Fund [IMF] and the OECD have also rediscovered the topic of inequality. In its World Economic Outlook of October last year, the IMF studied the relationship between globalisation and inequality. The OECD's Employment Outlook concluded last year that the trend of outsourcing and offshoring is increasing the vulnerability of jobs and wages in many developed nations. In the North-South context, debate previously revolved around the question of whether it is only inequality that is growing, or whether poverty is growing too. Poverty levels can in fact decrease in spite of growing inequality—if all incomes rise, for instance, but the higher income brackets do so faster than the lower ones. If this were the case, then growing inequality would be compatible with the Millennium [Development] Goals.

The latest World Bank review of purchasing power parities (PPPs) will, however, add fresh impetus to this debate. The data show that both global inequality and global poverty are vastly greater than previously assumed. It is reported that worldwide income inequality is not 65 Gini points, which would roughly equate to the level of South Africa, but 70 points. The Gini coefficient is a statistical measure of income distribution, with "0" corresponding to total equality and "100" to total inequality. An inequality level of 70 was never recorded before anywhere. The new PPP estimates also imply that the number of absolute poor is probably considerably higher than assessed so far. According to the outdated PPP calculations, 980 million people must do with less than the purchasing power of one dollar per day.

It is difficult to establish causal links between globalisation on the one hand and unemployment and inequality on the other. Many of the approaches used for doing so are questionable. For instance, the IMF outlook tried to ascertain what impact technological progress, financial globalisation and the international trade in goods have had on inequality. It concluded that technology and financial globalisation have boosted inequality, whereas international trade helped to reduce it by making goods and services cheaper.

## Trade and Technology

The difficulty, however, that it is hardly possible to assess these factors separately. Trade globalisation is inconceivable without technical progress, and the reverse is just as true. Technological change expresses itself in new forms of trade—such as the creation of global value chains or the provision of global call-centre services. Nonetheless, most researchers argue that free trade, one of the central pillars of globalisation, can only be blamed to a minimal extent for inequality and unemployment. For example, Robert Z. Lawrence argues that while more trade with developing countries caused greater inequality in the USA in the 1980s, its impact was negligible over the past ten years.

According to Lawrence, rising inequality and slow wage expansion—or even decline—are due to dramatic growth in profits and associated advantages for the top one percent of income earners in the USA. Any policy focusing merely on regulating trade would, therefore, be too narrow and unlikely to succeed. Instead, Lawrence calls for a change in taxation regimes and for lending state assistance to those who need to adapt to structural change. Lawrence's prominent colleague Paul Krugman, however, warns against underestimating the trade-related downward pressure on wages and labour relations in the USA. He points out that the USA used to import oil and other raw materials from the third world and manufactured goods from other industrialised regions like Canada, Europe and Japan. Today, however, the USA imports more manufactured goods from poor nations than from rich ones.

Krugman himself used to warn against exaggerated fears of globalisation. In the early 1990s, he pointed out that the imports of finished goods from the third world made up a relatively modest share of US gross domestic product (GDP). Today, he claims that the pressure on jobs and wages is probably not quite as modest as it was. Krugman estimates that the amount of manufactured goods imported from the third world has grown dramatically—from only 2.5% of US GDP in 1990 to six percent in 2006. Countries with very low wages registered the greatest export boost. As Krugman explains, in South Korea, Taiwan, Hong Kong and Singapore, the first "newly-industrialised countries," wages in 1990 were about 25% of the US level. Since then, however US imports are increasingly being sourced in Mexico, where wages are about 11% of the US level, and China, where they are only three or four percent. According to Krugman, only a minority of highly educated US employees has benefited from the growing trade with third world economies, greatly outnumbered by the losers.

---

*Not only do small minorities have no share in the benefits of globalisation—the vast majority of people misses out.*

---

## The Vast Majority Misses Out

This last point is crucial. Not only do small minorities have no share in the benefits of globalisation—the vast majority of people misses out. No serious observer will claim that globalisation, trade and international investment are not good for national economies in themselves. Yet even in the conservative camp, fears are mounting that only a tiny group at the top of society is reaping the benefits. Incidentally, this applies equally to the advanced countries and many developing countries, although details differ, of course. In any case, the question of appropriate counterstrategies and remedies is becoming urgent. Adjustment assistance for those negatively affected by globalisation is considered a rather conventional remedy in the rich world. The focus can be on reforming labour law, improving social-security systems or new measures for retraining and education. Such programmes are usually sold as "helping people to adapt to globalisation", although the measures used usually have only an aftercare character, without tackling the roots of unemployment and poverty.

That is precisely why Scheve and Slaughter are demanding drastic redistribution from the top down. In their ... article, they suggest abolishing all income tax for workers who earn less than the average national income, and drastically increasing the taxation rate for the top earners. Lawrence Summers, a former World Bank chief economist and former US treasury secretary, supported their call in the *Financial Times* by stating that to prevent protectionist tendencies, which would cut the overall benefits of globalisation, it was better to share the cake more fairly.

# Globalization Threatens Democracy and Promotes Economic Polarization

*Roger Bybee*

*Roger Bybee is a Milwaukee-based activist and writer.*

More and more, it is becoming clear that the essence of corporate globalization is to use capital's mobility to evade the constraints of democracy at the national level and establish rules that guarantee global corporate supremacy. Transnational corporations have come closer to being able to shift production sites whenever democracy threatens near-absolute corporate dominance.

## Anti-Globalization Sentiment

Trade agreements like NAFTA [North American Free Trade Agreement] have effectively given corporations the power to set rules and ignore laws on product safety and the environment, allowing them to override democratically enacted laws and even win damages for lost profits through decisions by remote and secretive non-elected panels. For example, the state of California stands to lose over $970 million for banning a Canadian-made gasoline additive called MTBE [methyl tertiary butyl ether] that made drinking water toxic and severely reduced the value of numerous homes.

However, the three-decade triumph of corporate globalization over democracy may now be facing its most broadly based and deeply felt challenge in the United States. The combination of falling wages, shrinking benefits, rising insecurity about both work and retirement, and the incessant flow of family-supporting jobs to China and Mexico have ignited a

Roger Bybee, "Globalization vs. Democracy: Are U.S. Victims Ready to Strike Back?" *Z Magazine*, vol. 21, November 2008. Reproduced by permission of the author.

grassroots rebellion. This anti-globalization sentiment currently takes much less dramatic form than the massive and militant streets protests of the 1999 "battle of Seattle" and elsewhere. Instead of fiery street protests, the new mood against globalization is most visible in polling results and the manner in which primary candidates have been compelled to adopt increasingly vocal positions against NAFTA-style trade agreements and corporate greed.

## False Premises, False Promises

Globalization's chief impresario, author and *New York Times* columnist Thomas Friedman, has claimed that if nations want to become competitive and attain prosperity, it means donning what he cheerfully calls the "golden straitjacket," that is accepting a regime of low wages, privatization, and deregulation to encourage the vitality of the unbridled free market and unlock prosperity for the entire society. True, "an expanding economy means shrinking your politics," he admits.

Particularly breathtaking is the level of economic polarization occurring under globalization. The richest 1 percent of Americans now collect 18.1 percent of total income, earning a much larger share of income than the bottom 40 percent of households, which only received 12.5 percent, a 2007 Congressional Budget Office study found.

---

*"Free trade" is a formula for lost jobs, falling wages, and economic insecurity.*

---

In Mexico a similar process of polarization has occurred. Wages have fallen at least 25 percent, according to a Carnegie Endowment [for International Peace] study. Low wages in Mexico (typically 60 cents to $1 an hour in U.S.-owned maquiladora plants) have exerted a strong allure to U.S. corporations, with over one million jobs lost since NAFTA's enactment, according to the Economic Policy Institute. At the same time, the removal of protections for Mexico's agricultural and retail industries, accompanied by the aggressive entry of U.S.-subsidized agribusiness products, has driven some 1.5 to 2 million farmers off the land. While low-wage employment in maquiladora plants along the border mushroomed after NAFTA's enactment, Mexico is now being increasingly bypassed in favor of even more repressive and lower-waged China.

## The Failure of Free Trade

The incorporation of China into the "free trade" regime, championed by both Democratic and Republican U.S. administrations, has created even more economic and social havoc than NAFTA. According to Robert Scott of the Economic Policy Institute: "Contrary to the predictions of its supporters, China's entry into the World Trade Organization (WTO) has failed to reduce its trade surplus with the United States or increase overall U.S. employment. The rise in the U.S. trade deficit with China between 1997 and 2006 has displaced production that could have supported 2,166,000 U.S. jobs. Most of these jobs (1.8 million) have been lost since China entered the WTO in 2001."

Meanwhile, deindustrialization and community decay has persuaded most Americans that "free trade" is a formula for lost jobs, falling wages, and economic insecurity. Moreover, this form of corporate globalization has corrosive impacts on the social fabric of communities abandoned by major corporations, with shattered lives—in the form of suicides, family breakups, physical abuse, criminality, and alcohol and drug abuse—following in the wake of shuttered plants, as Dr. Harvey Brenner has documented in his studies of unemployment.

# Is Globalization of the World Economy Good for the United States?

# Overview: Perceptions of Globalization in the United States

*Cletus C. Coughlin*

*Cletus C. Coughlin is vice president and deputy director of research at the Federal Reserve Bank of St. Louis.*

The issue of job security inevitably arises in any discussion about reducing international trade barriers. In 2006 the Chicago Council on Global Affairs and a number or partners surveyed public perceptions in the United States, China, India, and South Korea on a wide range of foreign policy issues.[1] Overall, the opinions expressed reveal similarities concerning the importance of protecting jobs as well as differences concerning the connection between international trade and job security. Specifically, responses from the U.S. survey help explain why international trade legislation in the United States is so controversial.

According to the 2006 survey, the American public feels that protecting the jobs of American workers should be the top U.S. foreign policy goal. The next three goals are preventing the spread of nuclear weapons, combating international terrorism, and securing adequate supplies of energy. In fact, the goal of protecting American jobs has been at or near the top of this survey's responses for more than twenty years.

The U.S. respondents see international trade as threatening American jobs. Although the majority of those surveyed think that international trade improves their standard of living, 67

---

1. Australia and Japan also participated. See www.thechicagocouncil.org/dynamic _page.php?id=56.

Cletus C. Coughlin, "Where You Live Affects What You Think about Trade," *International Economic Trends*, May 2007. © 2009 Federal Reserve Bank of St. Louis. Reproduced by permission.

percent of those surveyed also think that international trade adversely affects job security for American workers. Only 30 percent think international trade enhances job security.

Much job insecurity in the United States can be traced to the near doubling of the global pool of labor stemming from the integration of China and India into the world economy. China has become a major player in the export of manufactured goods, while India has become a major force in services. Perhaps surprisingly, this concern about job security does not translate into a desire for higher trade barriers. Although 36 percent do favor protectionism, 43 percent favor agreements that lower trade barriers so long as governmental assistance is provided to those who lose their jobs. An additional 15 percent would lower trade barriers without governmental assistance.

Like U.S. respondents, respondents in the Asian countries believe that protecting jobs in their countries should be a high priority for foreign policy. In China, protecting jobs was the highest-ranked foreign-policy priority; in South Korea, it was second behind promoting economic growth; and in India it was in a three-way tie with promoting economic growth and combating world hunger. A key contrast between these three Asian countries and the United States involves their perception of the connection between international trade and job security. Recall that less than one-third of the American public believes that international trade contributes to job security. Meanwhile, the comparable percentages in India (49 percent) and South Korea (51 percent) are roughly one-half and the percentage in China (65 percent) is nearly two-thirds. Thus, Asians are much more inclined to believe that trade contributes to job security than job insecurity.

Although job security is not the only consideration that influences the public's position on trade liberalization, it certainly plays an important role. A comparison of American views with Chinese views on the desirability of free trade agreements provides some suggestive evidence on this claim. For example, the percentage of Americans who believe their country should have a free trade agreement with China, India, and South Korea was 34 percent, 36 percent, and 39 percent, respectively. Such a reluctance to support free trade agreements likely reflects concerns that freer trade will increase job insecurity. Meanwhile, the percentage of Chinese who think their country should have a free trade agreement with the United States, India, and South Korea was 66 percent, 59 percent, and 66 percent, respectively.

The survey results point to the following conclusion: Because jobs are very important, political support for trade liberalization will increase if the costs borne by those who are adversely affected are mitigated. The majority (62 percent) of respondents to a September 2006 survey by the German Marshall Fund of the United States, however, believe that the U.S. government does a poor job in helping workers adjust to new competition.[2] In today's political reality in the United States, without effective mitigation, the potential gains from trade liberalization are quite likely to remain unrealized.

2. See www.gmfus.org/doc/GMF_TradeSurvey%202006.pdf.

# Americans Have Benefited from Globalization as Workers and Consumers

*Daniella Markheim*

*Daniella Markheim is the Jay Van Andel Senior Analyst in Trade Policy at the Heritage Foundation's Center for International Trade and Economics.*

A central theme in Barack Obama's campaign platform—and potentially in the president-elect's trade agenda—is the belief that free trade policies have been unfair to U.S. workers and businesses.

## Foreign Competition

The essence of the argument is that because foreign workers are willing to work for lower wages than their U.S. counterparts, and because the underdeveloped societies in which they live do not have the same levels of environmental protection or labor standards that U.S. citizens enjoy, foreigners should not be allowed to freely compete in U.S. markets. They can sell their products here but only if the U.S. government raises the price of the imports to the level that U.S. firms want to charge. In other words, they can sell, but they cannot compete on price.

It is true that U.S. trade commitments to lower tariffs and other trade barriers have exposed some of America's producers to foreign competition, and in some cases even driving them out of the marketplace. In many more cases, however, U.S. firms have responded by improving their products and their production processes. The benefits for U.S. citizens have

Daniella Markheim, "Free Trade: The Fairest Trade Policy for America," *Heritage Foundation WebMemo*, no. 2169, December 12, 2008. Copyright © 2008 The Heritage Foundation. Reproduced by permission.

been two-fold. In their capacity as workers, they have commanded increased wages on the basis of their increased efficiency and productivity. In their capacity as consumers, they have benefited from the availability of better products at cheaper prices.

## The Fair Trade Arguments

The special interest groups, lobbyists, and other proponents of so-called "fair trade" want to stop this process of improvement, demanding instead costly protectionist policies to prop up uncompetitive firms. Historically, the U.S. government raised prices of imports through the imposition of tariffs. Sometimes quotas were used to limit supply and drive up the price of imports indirectly.

These days, advocates of "fair trade" seek to drive up the price of imports by requiring foreign governments to raise their cost of production through their own regulatory process. They do this by threatening tariffs or quotas unless foreign governments adopt more restrictive—and costly—labor, environmental, and other standards. Rather than encouraging American firms to improve, the champions of "fair trade" would bolster America's competitiveness by making foreign producers less so.

---

*Policy makers should continue to liberalize trade with the open market policies that have been an instrumental part of America's economic success and dominance in the world markets.*

---

Unfortunately, this tactic will only make it harder for the United States to open markets around the world for U.S. exports and prevent America from enjoying the lower prices and better use of resources that stem from reducing trade barriers. It is true that there can be unfair foreign competition that can harm domestic business; however, there are mechanisms in place in U.S. free trade agreements (FTAs) and within the World Trade Organization designed to address these problems. Trade liberalization has opened markets around the world to U.S. goods and services, created higher-paying jobs for Americans, and attracted the investment needed for long-term economic growth. America cannot afford to abandon open market policies.

Internationally uncompetitive corporate tax rates, rigidities in the labor market, corruption, and other policy failures often add to the cost of freer trade—costs that erecting barriers to trade will not reduce. Making U.S. trade policy tougher and trade agreements harder to negotiate will not boost America's ability to compete in the global market. Instead, policy makers should continue to liberalize trade with the open market policies that have been an instrumental part of America's economic success and dominance in world markets.

## Fair Trade Is Unfair

Adding more restrictive labor, environmental, and other standards to the structure of America's trade agreements could eliminate the benefits that partner countries receive from free trade agreements with America. This would especially affect developing countries that use U.S. FTAs to advance domestic economic reforms and to lessen poverty. Demanding that developing countries implement and enforce U.S.-style regulations when many are struggling to create the very institutions needed to facilitate a healthy economy will not be successful—especially if these countries are denied access to the world's most important market and the economic growth that comes from that trade.

Keeping America's trade partners mired in poverty will do little to advance sound standards around the world and little to boost the U.S. and global economies. Historically, as a nation's prosperity increases, the desire—and more importantly, the ability—to adopt labor and environmental protections become stronger, resulting in policies that accommodate the individual needs of the country. Engaging in freer trade can better promote the evolution of good regulations by empowering countries with the economic opportunity to develop and raise living standards.

Moreover, making more stringent standards a part of trade agreements will not make freer trade "fairer" for America. Any negative consequences of freer trade—usually thought of as lost jobs or market share—are generally the result of inappropriate policies, not trade liberalization. Even in a country with relatively low tariffs and few investment restrictions, the interplay of tax, regulatory, labor, and other economic policies with relatively free flows of goods and capital can lessen or even negate the benefits of an open market.

---

*Free trade is one of the greatest economic engines of change, inspiring innovation and bolstering growth.*

---

## Free Trade Is Fair

The major economic benefits of free trade derive from the differences among trading partners, which allow any country embracing world markets a chance to become competitive. Free trade is fair when countries with different advantages are allowed to trade and capitalize on those differences.

Low wage costs, access to cheap capital, a highly skilled workforce, and other fundamental variables all play a role in determining what comparative advantage one country has over another in the global marketplace. Equalizing those differences in the name of "fairness" only negates or reduces a country's ability to benefit from participating in the global trade system.

Free trade allows a country to compete in the global market according to its fundamental economic strengths and to reap the productivity and efficiency gains that promote long-run wealth and prosperity. Indeed, there is no distinction between free trade and truly fair trade, and U.S. free trade policy should continue to support that ideal.

Embracing and taking advantage of globalization relies not just on free trade policies but on redressing the factors that lead to less competitive firms and workers in the first place. High U.S. corporate tax rates, complex and inefficient jobs and retraining programs, costly regulations, weak protection of property rights around the world, and other policy failures are the real threats to American competitiveness—issues that erecting trade barriers through "fair" trade policies will not resolve. Free trade is one of the greatest economic engines of change, inspiring innovation and bolstering growth. By keeping America open to trade, the new administration can ensure that U.S. workers, consumers, and companies really get a fair shot to earn and keep their place at the top of the global marketplace.

# Decreased Barriers to Free Trade Are Not Bad for U.S. Workers

*Daniel Griswold*

*Daniel Griswold is director of the Center for Trade Policy Studies at the Cato Institute, a nonprofit public policy research foundation headquartered in Washington, DC.*

Trade is not about more jobs or fewer jobs, but about better jobs. Advocates of trade liberalization who claim that lower barriers boost the total number of jobs in our economy are as wrong as skeptics who argue that lower barriers mean fewer jobs. During the debate over NAFTA [North American Free Trade Agreement] in 1993, people on both sides were guilty of this fundamental mistake. Independent presidential candidate H. Ross Perot famously predicted that passage of the agreement would create "a giant sucking sound" as jobs and investment headed south across the border. Advocates of the agreement, including the Clinton White House, countered that NAFTA would create hundreds of thousands of net new jobs. Both sides were wrong to the extent they predicted a net change in jobs either way.

## Job Shifting

Trade does cause certain jobs to disappear, certain companies to go out of business, and certain sectors of the economy to shrink. That is what we would expect from increased competition, domestic as well as international. But trade as a rule does not affect the total number of jobs or the overall rate of employment or unemployment. Studies that claim that trade expansion, trade deficits, or trade agreements have caused the loss of some specific number of jobs during a certain period of time are misleading if they imply that today's economy has that many fewer jobs than it would have otherwise. Trade does not affect the total number of jobs in an economy for three reasons.

---

*The much misunderstood reality of comparative advantage means that our economy will always be globally competitive in a range of sectors.*

---

First, if workers, capital, and resources can shift within the domestic economy, jobs eliminated by import competition will quickly be replaced by jobs created elsewhere. Focusing merely on jobs lost because of imports ignores the offsetting jobs that trade and globalization create through other channels. One channel is expanding exports, as U.S. producers ramp up production to meet demand abroad as well as at home. Trade competition also reduces costs for U.S. producers by allowing them to buy raw materials, intermediate inputs, and capital machinery at lower, more competitive global prices. Lower producer costs translate into higher profits, attracting more investment and creating more employment in those sectors that benefit from open markets. Trade also delivers lower prices on imported consumer goods, giving households more money to spend on domestic goods and services, stimulating further employment gains. Globalization also means more international investment flowing into the United States. Inward foreign direct investment creates jobs by establishing foreign-owned production facilities in the United States, while inflows of financial capital create jobs by reducing long-term interest rates, thus promoting greater investment and job creation by domestic companies.

## Comparative Advantage

Second, the much misunderstood reality of comparative advantage means that our economy will always be globally competitive in a range of sectors. If we lose our competitive edge in one sector or industry, because of shifting technology and factor prices or the emergence of new global competitors, the competitive edge of other sectors will be enhanced. The insight of comparative advantage, first expounded by David Ricardo in 1817, is that a country will tend to export what it can make more efficiently relative to what else it could produce domestically given its own endowment of resources. Another country may (in theory, anyway) be able to produce everything at a lower per unit cost than we can produce domestically, but we can still gain from exchanging what each country is relatively most efficient at producing. If the United States loses its shoe industry to lower-cost global competition, the reality of comparative advantage means that we will likely gain competitiveness and export share in pharmaceuticals, civil aircraft, financial services, and other sectors where we are relatively more efficient than making shoes. We may lose call center jobs, where we are relatively less efficient, but gain jobs in financial analysis or computer engineering. American workers will always be relatively more productive in some sectors than others in the domestic economy, ensuring that we will always be competitive in a range of global export markets.

---

*Changes in trade flows have not determined the overall level of employment in the U.S. economy.*

---

## Counterbalancing Factors

Third, trade tends not to affect the overall number of jobs because of other, more powerful and counterbalancing factors in the broader economy such as monetary policy and foreign exchange rates. If a surge in imports did cause widespread layoffs in certain sectors, the resulting increase in unemployment would push the Federal Reserve to tilt toward a looser monetary policy and lower interest rates to stimulate the overall economy. Increased imports would also have the effect of pumping more dollars into international markets, causing the dollar to depreciate on foreign currency markets. A weaker dollar, in turn, would make U.S. exports more attractive, stimulating employment in export sectors while dampening demand for imports, thus offsetting initial job losses.

In the same way, if trade restrictions could somehow artificially stimulate employment in certain sectors, driving unemployment below its normal rate, the Federal Reserve would likely move in the opposite direction, tightening monetary policy and credit to prevent overheating and potential inflation. Higher interest rates, in turn, would cool other sectors of the economy, offsetting the initial job gains from protection. Higher barriers to imports would also constrict the number of dollars flowing into international markets, causing the dollar to appreciate above the exchange rate that would have prevailed without the trade barriers in place. The stronger dollar would dampen international demand for our exports and stimulate demand for imports, again offsetting any short-term employment gains in the protected sectors. For all those reasons, changes in trade flows have not determined the overall level of employment in the U.S. economy.

---

*An increasingly globalized U.S. economy is perfectly compatible with a growing number of jobs and full employment.*

---

## Overall Employment

Even the most cursory glance at the employment numbers during recent decades should dispel any fear that trade and globalization threaten overall employment. Across the decades, against a backdrop of rising levels of trade and repeated business cycles, a central truth has stood out: In the long run, job growth in the United States tends to track growth in the labor force. As new workers have entered the labor market, U.S. producers have found profitable ways of employing them. Job growth invariably reverses during recessions, but then catches back up with labor-force growth during expansions, driving the unemployment rate back down to a level consistent with "full employment."

In the past four decades, during a time of expanding trade and globalization, the U.S. workforce and total employment have each roughly doubled.... Total employment has closely followed labor-force growth. Since 1965, the number of people employed in the U.S. economy has increased from 71.1 million to 146.1 million, while the number in the civilian labor force has grown from 74.5 million to 153.2 million—both growing at an identical annual rate of 1.73 percent. Total employment will stall and even reverse during recessions, but will invariably resume its upward climb as the economy recovers. Despite fears of lost jobs, total employment in the U.S. economy has grown by 16.5 million since 1997, 46.8 million since 1980, and 75.0 million since 1965. After four decades of demographic upheaval, technological transformations, dramatically rising levels of trade, and half a dozen recessions and recoveries, the current [2007] unemployment rate of 4.6 percent is virtually the same as it was in 1965. Obviously, an increasingly globalized U.S. economy is perfectly compatible with a growing number of jobs and full employment.

## Trade's Small Role in Job Churn

Expanding international trade does eliminate a certain number of jobs each year. We often see that reality in the news media and sometimes in our own communities: an auto-parts supplier downsizes its workforce, an apparel factory closes its doors, a telecommunications firm outsources a call center to India. Affected workers are real people with bills to pay and dependents to support. But the number of people dislocated from their jobs each year because of shifting trade patterns is relatively small in America's dynamic market economy where "job churn" is a normal, healthy fact of life.

The number of workers who lose their jobs because of expanding trade, outsourcing, and businesses moving offshore probably falls in the range of 300,000 to 500,000 each year. The Economic Policy Institute [EPI], a left-of-center research organization in Washington, claimed in a 2001 paper that rising imports had eliminated 3 million "actual and potential jobs" from 1994 to 2000—an average of 500,000 per year. In a more recent study, EPI claimed that our economy lost 200,000 jobs a year just from trade with China in the past decade. Lori Kletzer, in a 2001 study for the Institute for International Economics, estimated that trade accounted for 320,000 job losses annually from 1979 to 1999. Even if we accept the highest of those figures, jobs lost because of expanding trade are a relatively small component of the underlying churn in the U.S. labor market.

Every year, the U.S. economy creates and destroys millions of jobs. According to the U.S. Department of Labor, an average of 32.1 million jobs were created and 30.4 million were eliminated annually between 1992 and 2006, creating an average annual net job gain of 1.7 million. About half the churn is seasonal, but the other half is permanent, meaning that each year about 15 million jobs disappear, never to be seen again. If changing flows of trade account for the loss of 500,000 jobs a year, trade would be responsible for about 3 percent of the overall churn in the labor market.

Job displacement because of expanding trade also appears small when compared to weekly filings for unemployment compensation. If the estimates of job losses from trade expansion are correct, about 10,000 workers lose their jobs in a typical week because of trade-related causes. That provides plenty of sound bites and television images for the critics of trade. And yet, in a typical week, even when the economy is humming, more than 300,000 people will file claims for unemployment insurance. By that yardstick as well, workers displaced by expanding trade account for only 3 percent of total displaced workers.

---

*There is nothing unique or disturbing about the fact that changes in international trade account for a small share of job displacement in the U.S. labor market.*

---

## Reasons for Job Displacement

What accounts for the other 97 percent of job turnover? Technology probably accounts for most permanent job displacement. For example, introduction of the personal computer 25 years ago has eliminated hundreds of thousands of jobs for typists, secretaries, and telephone operators. The daily newspaper business has seen venerable papers close their doors and hundreds of thousands of reporting, editing, and production positions eliminated because of the migration of readers and advertising to the Internet. Kodak, the camera company headquartered in Rochester, New York, has laid off 30,000 workers since 2004—not because of unfair trade by foreign competitors, but because of the proliferation of digital cameras and plunging sales of film. Tower Records shut down its U.S. stores and laid off workers, not because of imports, but because iPods and other digital-music devices have cut deeply into sales of compact discs.

Workers also lose their jobs because of changing consumer tastes and domestic market competition as one American company cuts into the market share of another. There is nothing unique or disturbing about the fact that changes in international trade account for a small share of job displacement in the U.S. labor market.

Trade, like technology, affects the type of jobs in our economy but not the total number. If workers and capital can move freely between states and between sectors, jobs lost in one area will tend to be replaced by jobs created in another. The overall number of jobs depends on the growth rate of the economy and labor force, business investment, the flexibility of employers to hire or lay off workers, and other broader factors. A nation open to the global economy can enjoy low unemployment, just as a country with a closed economy can suffer high unemployment, and vice versa. It is simply wrong to blame trade for causing a net loss of jobs or anything other than a small fraction of job displacement.

# Evidence Shows Globalization Is Good for the United States

*William H. Overholt*

*William H. Overholt is director of the Center for Asia Pacific Policy at the RAND Corporation, a nonprofit research center.*

Protectionists who characterize free trade as almost treasonous are on a crusade to build new barriers around America in an effort to keep jobs in and imports out.

Some have built careers around denouncing the evils of globalization. CNN commentator Lou Dobbs, for example, criticizes free trade on a regular basis on his nightly show and in his book *Exporting America: Why Corporate Greed Is Shipping American Jobs Overseas*. A promo for the book on the CNN Web site states: "The shipment of American jobs to cheap foreign labor markets threatens not only millions of workers and their families, but also the American way of life."

## The Charge of Inequality

The most serious critique of globalization is the charge that it promotes inequality, driving down U.S. wages while enriching millionaire corporate executives. This charge is partly true, but mostly false.

The true part is that within many countries, globalization has enhanced the wealth of business owners and managers while providing proportionately less wage growth for ordinary workers. It has done so by expanding the workforce participating in the modern world economy to include much of the populations of Eastern Europe, China and India.

As a result, millions of workers in the United States and Western Europe now face more competition than ever before

William H. Overholt, "Globalization's Unequal Discontents," *Washington Post*, December 21, 2006. Reproduced by permission of the author.

from others willing to work for far lower wages. Capital has not experienced a proportionate increase in competition, so the share of corporate profits has risen and the share of wages has fallen. The rich get richer, while incomes of workers as a whole go up as well, but more slowly.

Some manufacturing workers in the United States—such as those who labored in huge factories making basic steel—have suffered as they've seen their jobs leave America for low-wage countries. But for workers as a whole, the truth about globalization and inequality is the opposite of what the protectionists claim. There are three caveats to the steel workers' story and two larger perspectives on inequality.

## Job Losses in the United States

One caveat is that protectionists enormously exaggerate the negative effects of globalization by attributing virtually all manufacturing job losses to competition with China. We are told by union leaders and some politicians that America is exporting millions of jobs to China. This is absolutely untrue.

Scholarly studies show that most job losses in the United States are attributable to domestic causes such as increased domestic productivity. A few years ago it took 40 hours of labor to produce a car. Now it takes 15. That translates into a need for fewer workers. Protectionists who blame China for such job losses are being intellectually dishonest. In fact, both China and the United States have lost manufacturing jobs due to rising productivity, but China has lost ten times more—a decline of about 25 million Chinese jobs from over 54 million in 1994 to under 30 million ten years later.

## Standard of Living

A second caveat is that there are two ways to increase people's standard of living. One is to increase their wages. The other is to decrease prices so that they can buy more things with the same amount of money.

The ability to buy inexpensive, quality Chinese-made shoes and Japanese-made cars at lower prices disproportionately benefits lower income Americans. The Wall Street banker who pays $350 for Church's shoes benefits relatively little, but the janitor who buys shoes for $25, rather than $50, at Payless or Target or Wal-Mart benefits greatly.

---

*The protectionists never mention the jobs created and saved by globalization.*

---

Lower prices due to imports from China alone—ignoring all other similar results of globalization—probably raise the real incomes of lower income Americans by 5 to 10 percent. That's something no welfare program has ever accomplished.

## New Jobs

A third caveat is that the protectionists never mention the jobs created and saved by globalization. If General Motors avoids bankruptcy, as seems likely [General Motors filed for bankruptcy in 2009], one important reason will be the profits it has made by selling cars in China. The vast China market, and the ability of American corporations to expand and refine their operations though a division of labor with China, creates many high-level jobs in U.S. operations ranging in diversity from Motorola to IBM to Caterpillar to Boeing to farming.

The first of the larger perspectives on globalization is that open economies adjust faster to their real competitive advantages, allowing them to employ their own people. The most recent U.S. unemployment rate was 4.4 percent [in 2006]. France, along with other relatively protected economies, typically has twice as high a proportion of the population unemployed because their workers are stuck in inappropriate jobs.

Still more protected economies, like many in Latin America, often run much higher rates of unemployment—up to 40%. Economies more open than the United States—like Singapore and Hong Kong—historically run lower rates of unemployment.

The worst inequality is between families whose breadwinners have jobs and those who don't. Globalization minimizes that problem.

## The Decline in Global Inequality

Globalization has brought countries with about 3 billion people from subhuman conditions of life into modern standards of living with adequate food, basic shelter, modern clothing rather than rags, and life spans that are over 60 rather than under 45. (In the early 1950s China's life expectancy was 41 years, in 2005 it was 72.7 years. This is the greatest reduction of inequality that has happened in human history.)

In East Asia, this reduction of inequality has resulted from a wave of economic growth that has swept through Japan, Taiwan, South Korea, Thailand, Malaysia, and much of Indonesia. It is rapidly spreading across China, is well on the way in India and Vietnam and is coming to other countries around the world.

The world's fastest growth is occurring in some of its poorest countries, notably India, China and Indonesia. The middle-income countries are growing faster on average than the rich countries. In other words, global inequality is declining fast.

It is not surprising when workers in industries undergoing adjustment complain about the pain of change. For many families, prolonged unemployment can wipe out their savings, cost them their homes and turn their lives into a nightmare. The suffering of these families can't be ignored.

## Objective Analysis

But sound economics is based on facts grounded in objective analysis, not on emotion. Sometimes, what seems like a "common sense" solution is not really very sensible at all, as is seen with the arguments of the protectionists. Even the best of intentions can, in the end, bring about the worst of outcomes. The protectionists' proposed policies would sharply increase the agony of unemployment.

America will not benefit if an increasing number of opinion leaders and elected officials use exaggerated, partial views of inequality to try to lead us into a future of slower growth, higher unemployment and greater world tensions.

Instead, America and its leaders should focus on how the nation can use the rapidly expanding economy to assist individuals who have suffered from globalization to get the education, training and opportunities in new industries they need to benefit rather than suffer from globalization.

# The Majority of Americans Are Worse Off from Current Globalization

*Jeff Faux*

*Jeff Faux is founding president and distinguished fellow at the Economic Policy Institute, a nonprofit, Washington-based think tank.*

Competently managed, America's integration into the global economy can contribute to increasing living standards for workers in America and in the rest of the world. Unfortunately, the process is being tragically mismanaged, carried out not with a carefully considered plan but with a chaotic patchwork of international trade and investment agreements and policies increasingly unaccountable to any country's citizens.

In America, as elsewhere, the benefits of the current form of globalization have been concentrated among those at the top of the income and wealth ladder, while the costs have been paid by working families at the middle and the bottom. Real wages and benefits for the majority of workers are stagnant, jobs have been destroyed, and family and community life has been stressed and, at times, broken apart.

In the United States, the mismanaged policies of the last two decades have severely damaged the nation's competitiveness and plunged it into a spiral of trade deficits. To some extent the economic harm has been obscured by massive borrowing from the rest of the world, borrowing that is clearly unsustainable.

America urgently needs to reverse its course with a comprehensive strategy that matches the scope and depth of globalization's challenges.

## Global Integration, Not Just Trade

America has always traded with other nations. From the end of the Civil War to the 1970s the international share of the U.S. economy was modest, and exports and imports were generally in balance or showed a small surplus. But in the last 25 years, foreign trade has risen 700%, more than doubling as a share of gross domestic product to 28%. In 2006, the excess of imports over exports will reach some $900 billion—7% of GDP [gross domestic product].

This dramatic shift reflects more than simply an increased movement of goods and services between the United States and other nations. It reflects an unprecedented economic integration with the rest of the world that is blurring the very definition of the "American" economy.

American business is steadily moving finance, technology, production, and marketing beyond our borders. Some 50% of all U.S.-owned manufacturing production is now located in foreign countries, and 25% of the profits of U.S. multinational corporations are generated overseas—and the shares are rapidly growing.

---

*The rules of the global economy now give corporate property rights priority over human rights.*

---

To think of global integration as simply "more trade" is as much an error as it would have been to label the consolidation of the continental U.S. economy in the 19th century as simply more trade among the states. As Renato Ruggiero, the first director-general of the World Trade Organization (WTO), observed in 1995: "We are no longer writing the rules of interaction among separate national economies. We are writing the constitution of a single global economy."

## A New Global Economic Constitution

This new "constitution" is evolving from the increasing number of multinational agreements such as the North American

Free Trade Agreement (NAFTA) and the WTO, bilateral trade and investment deals, and the policies of institutions such as the International Monetary Fund (IMF) and the World Bank. The World Trade Organization, for example, enforces some 17 different agreements, only two of which directly concern trade. The others are primarily aimed at making domestic economic policies (e.g., financial regulation, privatization, product safety) conform to a single standard.

Unfortunately, this new global economic constitution primarily protects and promotes the interests of only one category of citizen—the global corporate investor. The rules of the global economy now give corporate property rights priority over human rights, undercutting the hard-won domestic social contract that has supported broadly shared prosperity in advanced societies and in some developing countries as well. The rules have encouraged and often imposed policies of privatization, deregulation, domestic austerity, and export-dependent growth on sovereign nations. They have denied governments the right to effectively regulate imported products produced by exploiting labor and the environment, while requiring governments to protect corporate patents and other intellectual property. And they give corporate investors extraordinary privileges to sue governments in secret tribunals.

---

*Successive U.S. governments have plunged American employers and workers into a global market governed by rules reminiscent of late 19th- century capitalism.*

---

The U.S. government is the leading advocate of the new rules, which have consistently traded away opportunities of Americans who produce goods and services in the United States in favor of access by multinational corporations to workers and financial markets in other countries.

The policies that make up the evolving "constitution of a single global economy" have not themselves created the global marketplace. Rather, the root causes are changes in transportation, information, and management technologies that, since the end of the Cold War, have doubled the available global labor force to three billion workers. Under any circumstances this process would have challenged American living standards and the survival of companies that produce here. But instead of managing the process carefully and controlling the opening of the U.S. economy in sync with strategies to maintain our competitiveness and protect real incomes, successive U.S. governments have plunged American employers and workers into a global market governed by rules reminiscent of late 19th-century capitalism.

## Corporations Over Country

The emergence of these perverse policies is no accident. As "American" corporations can increasingly get their workers, financing, components, finished products, and customers in other countries, they are less dependent on the economic health of those who live and work in the United States.

As individuals, Americans who manage and own global enterprises may be as concerned about their nation's future as anyone else. But institutionally, they are paid to worry about their corporations, not their country. For decades, they have been making the point themselves, quite openly. In the 1980s the chief executive officer of Dow Chemical said he yearned to place his headquarters on an island "beholden to no nation or society." In 1995, the CEO of the Ford Motor Company said: "Ford isn't even an American company, strictly speaking. We're global. We're investing all over the world. . . . Our managers are multinational. We teach them to think and act globally." In 2006, the CEO of Cisco Systems—poster company for the information economy—went a step further: "What we are trying to do is outline an entire strategy of becoming a Chinese company."

Ralph Gomory, former IBM executive and now president of the Alfred P. Sloan Foundation, notes that, "There is and can be fundamental conflict between the goals of the company and the goals of the country." Jeffrey Garten, a major architect of U.S. globalization policies and now dean of Yale Business School, observes that America "must adapt to the reality that U.S. multinationalists' goals may no longer dovetail with the national interest."

---

*Workers are receiving a shrinking share of the economic pie.*

---

But policy making has not caught up with this changed reality. Lobbyists for global corporate investors have been the most powerful influence on the way Washington has managed America's integration into the global economy. As a result, the policies that have guided this integration have systematically favored the interests of global investors over those of the typical American worker.

## The Broken Job Ladder

Since 1979, as trade has expanded, imports have grown faster than exports, directly displacing some 7 million jobs in America. The threat of jobs being shipped overseas has in turn translated into reduced wages and benefits and a general decline in the bargaining power of U.S. workers. A 2004 Gallup poll showed that 61% of Americans fear that they or someone close to them will lose a job because the employer is moving to another country. The threat to offshore production, real or exaggerated, gives employers substantial leverage over their employees.

Not surprisingly, workers are receiving a shrinking share of the economic pie. The gap between what workers produce and what they receive has dramatically widened: Between 1980 and 2005 productivity in the U.S. economy rose 71%, while the real compensation (including benefits) of nonsupervisory workers rose 4% (nonsupervisory employees make up about 80% of U.S. workers). In the tradable manufacturing sector, productivity rose 131% while compensation of nonsupervisors gained 7%.

Since the end of the last recession in 2001, the purchasing power of the typical American worker's weekly paycheck has dropped 3%. Among working males, real hourly wages are now [2007] about where they were in 1973.

---

*The American economy is not generating the promised good jobs.*

---

Economists differ in their estimates of precisely how much of the rise in wage stagnation and overall income inequality is attributable to imbalanced trade, but there is little doubt that it has been substantial. Research on the 1980s and early 1990s shows that trade flows alone account for 10–30% of the growth in wage inequality, with some major studies suggesting even greater contributions. Such estimates are sufficiently high by themselves to warrant attention, but even these understate the case. Moreover, they miss many of the ways that globalization influences other factors that are typically cited as contributing to wage inequality (e.g., de-unionization, the threats by employers to move jobs overseas, and the growing political influence of multinationals).

That trade will make the distribution of income worse is embedded in fundamental economic logic. When workers in a high-wage nation are thrown into competition with workers in less-developed countries, those at the bottom end of the wage ladder in the former will be relatively worse off and those at the top end better off.

## No American Advantage

Defenders of the present mode of globalization tend to dismiss this as a problem for a small number of unskilled workers. But globalization's "losers" extend way beyond the uneducated—and their ranks are growing. Twenty-five years ago, American workers were assured by the promoters of "free-trade" agreements that their better education and access to superior U.S. technology would allow them to produce more high-value-added products. Americans would move up the global wage ladder, while workers from other countries would get the vacated lower-wage jobs at the bottom. But when skilled, high-paid jobs began to disappear, American workers were told that they were not skilled and educated *enough*. The problem, they are now informed, is not the ill-considered policies, the problem is them. So if they want to maintain their living standards they have to become much more educated and productive and to work harder and longer hours. And if they can't, perhaps their children can.

Yet Americans are working longer and are certainly more educated. The share of the workforce with college degrees doubled from 15% in 1973 to 30% over the last three decades, while the share of high school dropouts fell from 29% to 10%. Still, the American economy is not generating the promised good jobs. Projections by the Bureau of Labor Statistics conclude that by 2014 the number of occupations filled by people with college degrees will rise by merely one percentage point—from 28% to 29%. The share of jobs for which college-level education is actually required is projected to be just 21%.

The evidence is overwhelming that what was once thought of as America's natural comparative advantage—skills, technology, and organization—can now be duplicated or even surpassed by other nations. Outsourcing offshore has now ratcheted up to jobs in research and development that Americans had assumed would always be ours because of our advanced technology, prestigious universities, and Nobel Prize–winning scientists. "American" transnationals are locating R&D [research and development] in India, Taiwan, and China, where the skills are high and come cheap. An analysis of 57 recent major research initiatives of the U.S. telecommunications industry showed that all but five were located outside the United States. According to one estimate, 80% of engineering tasks in product development can be "easily outsourced." Another suggests that as many as 60 million U.S. workers are vulnerable to having their jobs shipped to another country.

The notion that the U.S. economy can prosper by selling high-value services while the rest of the world sells us their goods is now clearly not credible. Manufacturing is our most important source of productivity and motivator of technological innovation. In fact, much of the jobs and wealth creation associated with the information economy are tied to the production of goods; success results from setting trained people to work on problems in the context of day-to-day production, whether autos or pharmaceuticals or Hollywood films. The more we offshore production, the harder it is to compete in the world on the basis of higher productivity and creativity.

## Job Insecurity

Princeton economist Alan Blinder, former vice chairman of the Federal Reserve Board, recently warned that "tens of millions of additional workers will start to experience an element of job insecurity that has heretofore been reserved for manufacturing workers. It is predictable that they will not like it."

The growing disconnect between many large American employers and their employees is further shredding the sense of mutual dependence that lies at the heart of a productive workplace. Employers who are searching the globe for cheaper labor have less incentive to invest in the long-term development of their U.S. labor force. And workers who are constantly threatened by offshoring have little reason to feel loyal to the firm. Again, these attitudes have spread beyond the sectors immediately impacted by trade and increasingly pervade the U.S. economy. As Thomas Kochan of MIT [Massachusetts

Institute of Technology] has observed, "employers have replaced the basic social contract at work—the norm that hard work, loyalty, and good performance will be rewarded with a good wage, dignity, and security—with a norm that gives primacy to cutting operating costs and obtaining the highest possible profit."

# Working Americans Have Suffered from the Effects of Globalization

*Stephen Lendman*

*Stephen Lendman is a writer and a research associate for the Centre for Research on Globalization.*

Globalized trade has a long history, but the notion of a globalized marketplace came into its own in the 1980s. It was hailed as a Western, mainly US, prescription for economic growth and prosperity lifting all boats. In fact, only yachts benefitted by design so the privileged could gain at the expense of all others preyed on.

The UN's International Labour Organization's (ILO) Commission on the Social Dimension of Globalization is comprised of representatives from labor, government and business. In 2004, it issued a damning appraisal of world trade rule's harm and the subsequent distress caused by unfair practices. It ranges from how TRIPS [agreement on Trade-Related Aspects of Intellectual Property Rights] prevents affordable generic lifesaving drugs being sold in developing countries to the shifting tax burden from business and the rich to workers, and much more.

## An Exodus of Jobs

In the US and West, the damage comes from exporting jobs and offshoring manufacturing and service operations to low-wage countries. It began in the late 1950s when modest numbers of them went to Canada to take advantage of the cost savings there. The pace then quickened in the 1960s and 1970s with the exodus of production jobs in autos, shoes, clothing,

Stephen Lendman, "The War on Working Americans—Part II," OpEdNews.com, August 29, 2007. Copyright © 2007, OpEdNews. Reproduced by permission.

cheap electronics, and toys as well as routine service work like credit card receipt processing, airline reservations and basic software code writing.

What started as simple assembly and service work early on, then took off in the 1980s. It spread up and down the value chain and now embraces almost any type good or service not needing a home-based location such as retail clerks, plumbers, and carpenters; top-secret defense research, design and selected types of manufacturing; and certain types of specialized activities companies so far have kept at home. What's moving abroad, however, is big business getting bigger with Gartner Research estimating outsourcing generated $298.5 billion in 2003 global revenues.

The toll adds up to a global race to the bottom in a country where services now account for 84% of the economy. The once bedrock manufacturing portion is just 10% and falling as more good jobs in it are lost in an unending drain. Since the start of 2000 alone, about one in six factory jobs, over three million in total, have been affected. The sector is less than a third of its size 40 years ago and one-fourth the peak it hit during WWII [World War II].

---

*Domestic job growth is stagnant.*

---

## The Future of U.S. Jobs

It's been devastating for the nation's 130 million working people. No longer are unions strong and workers well-paid with assured good benefits like full health insurance coverage and pensions. Today, all types of financial services comprise the largest economic sector. Much of it is in trillions of dollars of high stakes speculation annually producing wads of cash for elite insiders (when things go as planned) and nothing for the welfare of most others and the good of the country.

Worst of all is the poor and declining quality of most service sector jobs measured by wages, benefits, job security and overall working conditions. It's because fewer good ones exist, unions are weak, and workers are at the mercy of employers indifferent to their plight. People are forced to work longer and harder for less just to stay even. Jobs in this sector are mostly concentrated in unskilled or low-skill areas of retail, health care and temporary services of all kinds. They pay lots less than full-time jobs, and have few or no benefits and little prospect for future improvement. This all happened by design to crush worker rights and commoditize them like all other production inputs.

The Department of Labor now projects job categories with the greatest future expected growth are cashiers; waiters and waitresses; other restaurant-related workers; janitors and cleaning personnel; retail clerks; and child care workers—all low-skill areas. Harvard degrees aren't required. Neither are high school ones.

Most in-demand higher-skilled jobs are projected to be for nurses, post-secondary teachers and sales representatives. There are still plenty of high-tech jobs in areas like network systems and data analysis and software engineering applications and systems. But watch out. They're being lost as well to low-wage countries in an unending domestic job drain affecting all types of work able to be done anywhere. It shows why domestic job growth is stagnant (despite the hype it isn't), eligible workers are dropping out of the work force, and the decline is sure to continue unless legislation stops it. None is in sight or imagined.

## Outsourcing of Jobs

The loss of good well-paying jobs means fewer high-end and a range of low-skilled ones are all that remain for vast numbers of young people whose futures look bleak. Two research studies among others highlight the problem. One by University of California staffers in 2004 estimated up to 14 million American jobs are at risk to outsourcing, and another by Gartner Research predicts as many as 30% of high-tech jobs may be lost to low-wage countries by 2015. In addition, writing in the March/April 2006, issue of *Foreign Affairs* on what he calls a "third Industrial Revolution," former Federal Reserve vice chairman Alan Blinder estimated 28–42 million American service sector jobs are vulnerable and could be lost to foreign labor.

In low-wage countries, they're done at far less cost to US employers in their company-owned or subcontracted out operations. Blinder added starkly, "We have so far barely seen the tip of the offshoring iceberg, the eventual dimensions of which may be staggering." Veteran financial analyst and writer Bob Chapman calls this the "rape of our economy" with enormous, wrenching and destructive consequences to the lives of millions of working people pursuing an illusory American dream.

It affects the skilled and unskilled alike for all types of jobs at risk. Chapman cites India as an example noting once only low-skill and routine programming jobs went there. Now, he says, it's "software aeronautical engineers, banking, insurance, investment banking and drug research" along with many other high-end jobs where companies can hire skilled professionals at a fifth the cost of US and European ones. So why wouldn't they, and more are in a growing trend.

All types of financial jobs at all levels are also being eliminated with financial institutions moving sizeable chunks of investment banking, research, trading operations, and other professional jobs abroad for big cost savings. Deloitte & Touche estimates the industry will outsource 20% of its cost base by 2010 with more to come in a continuing job drain for big cost savings abroad. The ones lost will be in financial services and most other sectors in a trend looking like it won't end until the US is as low a wage nation as those now taking our jobs.

## A Fall in Workers' Standards of Living

Over the past 30 years, most people have seen an unprecedented fall in their standards of living. Adjusted for inflation, the average American worker now earns less than in the mid-1970s with the minimum wage unchanged at $5.15 an hour since 1997 until the 110th Congress raised it in pathetically small steps to a wholly inadequate top level. Beginning July 24, it rose to $5.85, will go to $6.55 July 24, 2008, and to $7.25 July 24, 2009. Until the increase, minimum worker pay was at the lowest point relative to average wages since 1949. It got many states, comprising over half the population, to raise their own, but it's not enough.

---

*Over the past 30 years, most people have seen an unprecedented fall in their standards of living.*

---

A recent study released by the Center for Economic and Policy Research (CEPR) shows the dire state of things. It reported about one in three jobs in the country, about 47 million of them, pay low wages (defined as two-thirds the median wage or $11.11 per hour or less) with few or no benefits like health insurance, pensions or retirement accounts. It's barely enough for a family of two adults and two children to exceed the official understated poverty level of $20,444 in 2006 (or $9.83 an hour), and by this definition one in four workers (35 million) only earned poverty-level wages. But millions of others fall below it because official statistics way understate the problem, and workers earning around $11.11 an hour in cities like New York, Chicago, Los Angeles and other large ones can't get by if they have to support a family on it.

## A Class Society by Design

These growing millions now comprise a permanent underclass in a nation unwilling to admit what census data and private research now show. America is a rigid class society by design with extreme wealth at the top, a declining (maybe dying) middle class, and a growing underclass of low-paid workers and poor, many desperately so.

Following the inequalities of the 1920s, the nation experienced what economic historians Claudia Goldin and Robert Margo called "the Great Compression." Income gaps narrowed from the positive effects of New Deal and Great Society programs, strong unions, and an equitable tax system for individuals and corporations. From then to now, call it "the Great Expansion" of inequality with the gap between rich and most others the greatest it's been since the Gilded Age of the "robber barons" and getting worse.

*BusinessWeek* magazine highlighted the trend in December 2003 and accompanying research. It showed a decline in social mobility over the past few decades. The article was called "Waking Up from the American Dream—Meritocracy and Equal Opportunity Are Fading Fast." It noted the "Wal-Martization" of the country corporate America embraces to control labor costs by outsourcing jobs, de-unionizing, hiring temps and part-timers, and dismantling internal career ladders to boost profits at the expense of people. What's left is a proliferation of dead-end, low-wage jobs with public policy skewed to keep it that way. It needs stressing again. This didn't happen by chance. It was by design to destroy organized labor, and so far it's working.

---

*While total reported income rose almost 9% in 2005, average incomes for the bottom 90% of the population dropped .6% from the previous year.*

---

## Poverty in America

In its most recent State of Working America—2006/2007, the Economic Policy Institute (EPI) reports the official poverty level in 2004 stood at 12.7% or 37 million people, including

13 million children. It also showed for the first time ever, poverty in the country grew in the first three years of an economic recovery. In its study, EPI cited factors today they call "historically unique":

- increased globalized trade;

- low union membership;

- more low-skilled and high-skilled immigration; and

- fewer favorable social norms guiding employer behavior to provide "adequate safety nets, pensions, and health care arrangements."

EPI noted the biggest challenge in today's "new economy" isn't (macro) growth but how benefits get distributed with such a high proportion skewed upward.

Left out entirely are the 16 million [that] 2005 census figures show are on the very bottom living in "extreme" poverty that's defined as a family of four with an annual income of $9,903 or less. Even more disturbing is how fast the poverty rate is increasing. The numbers of those worst off grew by 26% from 2000–2005 or 56% faster than for the total poverty population. Further, it happened mostly in years of economic expansion after the 2001 recession ended late that year. Notable also is the disturbing decline in higher-paying jobs leaving what's left for unskilled or low-skill workers. They pay pitiful wages and few, if any, benefits with crumbling social safety net protection left to pick up the slack.

The Oakland Institute policy think tank promotes social and economic justice. It recently reported its disturbing assessment of things saying 10% of the US population (around 30 million) "experiences hunger or is at risk of going hungry." A December 2006, Helsinki-based World Institute for Development Economics Research of the UN [United Nations] University study also reported disturbing findings. They showed the richest 1% of adults owned 40% of global assets in 2000, and the richest 10% held 85% of them.

EPI reported the top 1% controls more than one-third of America's wealth, the bottom 80% has 15.3%, and the top 20% holds 84.7% of it. In contrast, the poorest 20% are in debt and owe more than they own. Globalization, automation, outsourcing, the shift from manufacturing to services, weak unions, deregulation, and other harmful economic factors all add to the problem.

## Growing Inequality

Other data show an astonishing generational shift of well over $1 trillion of national wealth annually from 90 million US working class households to for-profit corporations and the richest 1% of the population. It created what economist Paul Krugman calls an unprecedented wealth disparity getting worse that shames the nation and is destroying the bedrock middle class without which democracy can't survive.

A similar conclusion also came from an analysis of income tax data by Professor Emmanuel Saez of the University of California-Berkeley and Professor Thomas Piketty of the Paris School of Economics. Both men are noted for their work on income inequality. Their research found the top 1% of Americans in 2005 (about 3 million people) got their largest share of national income since 1928—21.8%, up from 19.8% a year ago or a 10% gain. Further, the top 10% received 48.5% of all reported income in 2005, also the highest level since 1928, up 2% from 2004, and one-third since the late 1970s.

The top one-tenth of 1% (about 300,000 people) did best of all, to no surprise. It got as much income in total as the bottom 150 million Americans combined. In addition, while total reported income rose almost 9% in 2005, average incomes for the bottom 90% of the population dropped .6% from the previous year.

## Corporate Welfare

Further, the Bush administration tax cuts for the wealthy greatly widened the income gap between rich and poor that was the whole idea behind them with a healthy piece of the benefits going to big corporations. In the 1950s, they contributed an average of 28% to federal revenues. That dropped to 21% in the 1960s and about 10% and falling since the 1980s. It's happening with the corporate tax rate at 35%, but few of the giants pay it. According to the Government Accountability Office (GAO), 94% of major corporations now pay less than 5% of their income in taxes, and corporate tax payments overall are at their lowest level in 60 years. In addition, many large companies pay no tax, and some end up with sizable rebates on top of huge corporate welfare subsidies under a system of socialism for big corporations and the rich and "free market" capitalism for the rest of us.

Saez and Piketty also reported their findings may be understated because the wealthy are more likely to file late tax returns so those who did weren't included in the study. Also, the IRS [Internal Revenue Service] acknowledges it can account for only about 70% of business and investment income, most, of course, going to high-income earners. What's missing is $300–$400 billion a year that adds up to trillions of untaxed dollars for the rich with the rest of us having to make up for it.

Recent US Commerce Department data is also disturbing. It shows the share of national income going to wages and salaries the lowest on record with their data going back to 1929. And the Center on Budget and Policy Priorities (CBPP) finds wage and salary growth in the current recovery growing at half the average rate for post-recessionary periods since the end of WWII while corporate profits in the current period grew over 50% more than the post–WWII average. It's the first time on record, corporate profits got a larger share of income growth in a recovery than wages and salaries—46% to 34%.

# Organizations to Contact

*The editors have compiled the following list of organizations concerned with the issues debated in this book. The descriptions are derived from materials provided by the organizations. All have publications or information available for interested readers. The list was compiled on the date of publication of the present volume; the information provided here may change. Be aware that many organizations take several weeks or longer to respond to inquiries, so allow as much time as possible.*

**American Enterprise Institute for Public Policy Research (AEI)**
1150 Seventeenth Street NW, Washington, DC   20036
(202) 862-5800 • fax: (202) 862-7177
e-mail: info@aei.org
Web site: www.aei.org

The American Enterprise Institute for Public Policy Research (AEI) is a private, nonpartisan, nonprofit institution dedicated to research and education on issues of government, politics, economics, and social welfare. AEI sponsors research and publishes materials defending the principles and improving the institutions of American freedom and democratic capitalism. AEI publishes the *American*, a bimonthly magazine, and a series of papers on the topic of economics in its Economic Outlook series.

**Cato Institute**
1000 Massachusetts Avenue NW
Washington, DC   20001-5403
(202) 842-0200 • fax: (202) 842-3490
Web site: www.cato.org

The Cato Institute is a public policy research foundation dedicated to limiting the role of government, protecting individual liberties, and promoting free markets. The Cato Institute works to originate, advocate, promote, and disseminate applicable policy proposals that create free, open, and civil societies in the United States and throughout the world. Among the Cato Institute's publications is the book by Johan Norberg, *Financial Fiasco: How America's Infatuation with Homeownership and Easy Money Created the Economic Crisis.*

## Centre for Economic Policy Research (CEPR)

53-56 Great Sutton Street, London   EC1V 0DG
   United Kingdom
+44 (0)20 7183 8801 • fax: +44 (0)20 7183 8820
e-mail: cepr@cepr.org
Web site: www.cepr.org

The Centre for Economic Policy Research (CEPR) is the leading European research network in economics. CEPR conducts research through a network of academic researchers and disseminates the results to the private sector and policy community. CEPR produces a wide range of reports, books, and conference volumes each year, including *The First Global Financial Crisis of the 21st Century.*

## Economic Policy Institute (EPI)

1333 H Street NW, Suite 300, East Tower
Washington, DC   20005-4707
(202) 775-8810 • fax: (202) 775-0819
e-mail: epi@epi.org
Web site: www.epi.org

The Economic Policy Institute (EPI) is a nonprofit Washington-based think tank that seeks to broaden the discussion about economic policy to include the interests of low- and middle-income workers. EPI briefs policy makers at all levels of government; provides technical support to national, state, and local activists and community organizations; testifies before national, state, and local legislatures; and provides information and background to the print and electronic media. EPI publishes books, studies, issue briefs, popular education materials, and other publications, among which is the biennially published *The State of Working America.*

**Global Policy Forum (GPF)**
777 UN Plaza, Suite 3D, New York, NY   10017
(212) 557-3161 • fax: (212) 557-3165
e-mail: gpf@globalpolicy.org
Web site: www.globalpolicy.org

Global Policy Forum (GPF) is a nonprofit organization with consultative status at the United Nations (UN). The mission of GPF is to monitor policy making at the UN, promote accountability of global decisions, educate and mobilize for global citizen participation, and advocate on vital issues of international peace and justice. GPF publishes policy papers, articles, and statements, including the briefing paper, "The Precarious State of Public Finance."

**International Monetary Fund (IMF)**
700 Nineteenth Street NW, Washington, DC   20431
(202) 623-7000 • fax: (202) 623-4661
e-mail: publicaffairs@imf.org
Web site: www.imf.org

The International Monetary Fund (IMF) is an organization of 186 countries, working to foster global monetary cooperation, secure financial stability, facilitate international trade, promote high employment and sustainable economic growth, and reduce poverty around the world. The IMF monitors the world's economies, lends to members in economic difficulty, and provides technical assistance. The IMF publishes fact sheets, reports on key issues, and the *IMF Annual Report.*

**Peterson Institute for International Economics**
1750 Massachusetts Avenue NW
Washington, DC   20036-1903
(202) 328-9000 • fax: (202) 659-3225
e-mail: comments@petersoninstitute.org
Web site: www.iie.com

The Peterson Institute for International Economics is a private, nonprofit, nonpartisan research institution devoted to the study of international economic policy. The institute seeks to provide timely and objective analysis of and concrete solutions to a wide range of international economic problems. The institute publishes numerous policy briefs available on its Web site, including "Islam, Globalization, and Economic Performance in the Middle East."

## World Economic Forum
3 East Fifty-Fourth Street, 17th Floor
New York, New York   10022
(212) 703-2300 • fax: (212) 703-2399
e-mail: contact@weforum.org
Web site: www.weforum.org

The World Economic Forum is an independent international organization committed to improving the state of the world by engaging leaders in partnerships to shape global, regional, and industry agendas. The World Economic Forum has no political or national interests, and holds annual meetings among world leaders. The World Economic Forum publishes annual, global risk, and events reports, including "The Global Agenda 2009."

## World Trade Organization (WTO)
Centre William Rappard, Rue de Lausanne 154
Geneva 21   CH-1211
    Switzerland
(41-22) 739 51 11 • fax: (41-22) 731 42 06
e-mail: enquiries@wto.org
Web site: www.wto.org

The World Trade Organization (WTO) is the only global international organization dealing with the rules of trade between nations, with the goal of helping producers of goods and services, exporters, and importers conduct their business. The WTO sponsors trade agreements between member nations and supports trade liberalization. Among the information available on its Web site are the regional trade agreements, including the North American Free Trade Agreement (NAFTA).

## Worldwatch Institute

1776 Massachusetts Avenue NW, Washington, DC   20036
(202) 452-1999 • fax: (202) 296-7365
e-mail: worldwatch@worldwatch.org
Web site: www.worldwatch.org

The Worldwatch Institute's mission is to generate and promote insights and ideas that empower decision makers to build an ecologically sustainable society that meets human needs. The institute seeks innovative solutions to intractable problems, emphasizing a blend of government leadership, private sector enterprise, and citizen action that can make a sustainable future a reality. The institute publishes *World Watch* magazine and numerous reports, including "Powering China's Development."

# Bibliography

## Books

C. Fred Bergsten, ed. *The United States and the World Economy: Foreign Economic Policy for the Next Decade.* Washington, DC: Peterson Institute for International Economics, 2005.

Jagdish Bhagwati *In Defense of Globalization.* New York: Oxford University Press, 2007.

Daniel Cohen *Globalization and Its Enemies.* Trans. Jessica B. Baker. Cambridge, MA: MIT Press, 2006.

Peter Dicken *Global Shift: Mapping the Changing Contours of the World Economy.* New York: Guilford Press, 2007.

Wayne Ellwood *The No-Nonsense Guide to Globalization.* Toronto, ON: New Internationalist Publications: 2006.

Franklin Foer *How Soccer Explains the World: An Unlikely Theory of Globalization.* New York: HarperCollins, 2004.

Thomas L. Friedman *The World Is Flat: A Brief History of the Twenty-First Century.* New York: Farrar, Straus and Giroux, 2007.

Lui F. Hebron and John F. Stack Jr. *Globalization: Debunking the Myths.* Upper Saddle River, NJ: Pearson Prentice Hall, 2008.

John M. Hobson and Leonard Seabrooke, eds.  *Everyday Politics of the World Economy.* New York: Cambridge University Press, 2007.

Paul Krugman  *The Return of Depression Economics and the Crisis of 2008.* New York: W.W. Norton, 2009.

Kenneth Pomeranz and Steven Topik  *The World That Trade Created: Society, Culture, and the World Economy, 1400 to the Present.* Armonk, NY: M.E. Sharpe, 2006.

Jeffrey D. Sachs  *The End of Poverty: Economic Possibilities for Our Time.* New York: Penguin Press, 2005.

Manfred B. Steger  *Globalization: A Very Short Introduction.* New York: Oxford University Press, 2009.

Joseph E. Stiglitz  *Making Globalization Work.* New York: W.W. Norton, 2007.

Martin Wolf  *Why Globalization Works.* New Haven, CT: Yale University Press, 2004.

Beth V. Yarbrough and Robert M. Yarbrough  *The World Economy: International Trade.* Mason, OH: Thomson/South-Western, 2006.

# Periodicals

Ronald Bailey — "The Poor May Not Be Getting Richer: But They Are Living Longer, Eating Better, and Learning to Read," *Reason Online*, March 9, 2005. www.reason.com.

Gary Becker and Kevin Murphy — "Do Not Let the 'Cure' Destroy Capitalism," *Financial Times*, March 19, 2009.

C. Fred Bergsten and Arvind Subramanian — "Globalizing the Crisis Response," *Washington Post*, October 8, 2008.

Jared Bernstein and Josh Bivens — "The Pain of Globalisation," *Guardian*, November 8, 2007.

Alan Blinder — "Offshoring: The Next Industrial Revolution?" *Foreign Affairs*, March-April 2006.

David Brooks — "The Cognitive Age," *New York Times*, May 2, 2008.

Bob Davis, John Lyons, and Andrew Batson — "Wealth of Nations: Globalization's Gains Come with a Price; While Poor Benefit, Inequality Feeds a Backlash Overseas," *Wall Street Journal*, May 24, 2007.

Mark Engler — "The World Is Not Flat," *Dollars & Sense*, May-June 2008.

Thomas L. Friedman — "Big Ideas and No Boundaries," *New York Times*, October 6, 2006.

Simon Johnson        "The Quiet Coup," *Atlantic*, May
                     2009.

Henry A.             "Falling Behind: Globalization and
Kissinger            Its Discontents," *International Herald
                     Tribune*, June 3, 2008.

Marc Levinson        "Freight Pain: The Rise and Fall of
                     Globalization," *Foreign Affairs*,
                     November-December 2008.

Will Marshall        "Curing Globaphobia," *Blueprint*,
                     January 4, 2007.

Branko Milanovic     "Developing Countries Worse Off
                     than Once Thought—Part I,"
                     *YaleGlobal Online*, February 11, 2008.
                     www.yaleglobal.yale.edu.

Rick Newman          "Why Bank Nationalization Is So
                     Scary," *U.S. News & World Report*,
                     February 22, 2009. www.usnews.com.

Sandra Polaski       "Winners and Losers: Impact of the
                     Doha Round on Developing
                     Countries," *Carnegie Endowment
                     Report*, March 2006.
                     www.carnegieendowment.org.

Raymond              "IMF Predicts Economy Worse than
Richman, Howard      World Economy in 2010," *American
Richman, and         Thinker*, April 30, 2009.
Jesse Richman        www.americanthinker.com.

Robert J.            "Globalization Is a Reality—Deal
Samuelson            with It," *Investor's Business Daily*,
                     October 24, 2007.

Sherle R.
Schwenninger

"Redoing Globalization," *Nation*, January 12, 2009.

Bill Steigerwald

"India Rising," *Pittsburgh Tribune-Review*, April 7, 2007.

Joseph E. Stiglitz

"A Progressive Response to Globalization," *Nation*, April 17, 2006.

Bruce Stokes

"China: A Rival but Not an Adversary," *National Journal*, May 9, 2009.

# Index